The Contemporary Political Economy of Islamic Thought

Professor Mohamed Kazem Al Mouhajer

Translated by Taj Al-Banna

First Edition

NEWMAN SPRINGS PUBLISHING
320 Broad Street
Red Bank, NJ 07701

First originally published by Newman Springs Publishing 2025

ISBN 979-8-89617-284-0 (Paperback)
ISBN 979-8-89617-285-7 (Digital)

Printed in the United States of America

In the name of Allah, the Most Gracious, the Most Merciful

To the soul of my grandfather, the diligent Allama Al Sheikh Habib Al Ibrahim Al Mouhajer, my source of inspiration, my faith pillar, and my knowledge fountain.

To my mother's gentle soul and to my dear sister, Hajja Fatima, who showed me the real meaning of patience and pure spirit.

To my beloved wife, Hajja Khadija, my sanctuary of strength and empowerment.

To my dear ones, just like my own, Amin, Yusra, Khaled, and Rahma, with whom my eyes rejoice.

To all of them, I dedicate the fruit of my intellectual endeavors.

Mohamed Kazem

Contents

Introduction

My academic journey in economics began in 1968 at the university and culminated in 1980 with completing my doctoral degree in economics from Humboldt University of Berlin. Subsequently, I embarked on my professional career, engaging in research, teaching, and the formulation of economic policies. This journey has provided me with a comprehensive understanding of various aspects of economics, whether in theoretical aspects or practical policies. The expansion of knowledge has been the key factor in shaping my perspective, my intellectual framework, and my vision of liberal economic thought with all its crises and policies that have led to the impoverishment of many nations around the world.

At the same time, the environment of faith and science in which I was raised, and the impact of my grandfather's esteemed Allama Sheikh Habib and his teachings, were the motives of my decent exposure to various aspects of Islamic thought.

The challenge grew in me with the advent of the new liberalism and its proclamation of the triumph of liberal thought and the "end of history." At that point, I truly sensed that my scholarly and religious duty compelled me to undertake serious research to derive Islamic economic thought from its intellectual perspective and to extract practical reasoning within the contexts of its application during specific historical stages. This emanates from my belief that it should be intrinsic, not dictated by the will of individuals, for where the self intertwines with the subject matter, it potentially loses some of its essence and brilliance.

However, the intensity of my professional duties prevented me from doing so; I only found the available opportunity after leaving my job in 2012. I ventured into an intensive effort, dedicating up to seven hours per day to reading and research without interruption.

In 2019, with my reliance on Allah and after matters were completed from all aspects, I initiated writing this scientific work, which was concluded in 2022 with the same effort and determination. And, thanks to God, it was the best of all my other scientific works, which surpass dozens of books and research papers, in terms of its depth and authenticity in the extrapolation of the Islamic economic thought. This scientific work raises the level of global economic thought of leading economists. I hope, by the will of the Creator, that I have fulfilled my scientific and religious duty with all my available capabilities.

And here I must express my appreciation and thanks to all those who assisted me in completing this work, especially the discussions I sometimes had with colleagues and faithful friends on specific topics of this book, notably Professor Mohsen Salih, Professor Muhammad Tayy, and Dr. Abdel Halim Fadlallah.

They have all my appreciation, thanks, and gratitude.

Also, I can only express my gratitude to my dearest friend Mohamed Khalil Skaine for the technical assistance he provided, which facilitated my work.

The greatest thanks and gratitude remain to my beloved wife, Hajja Khadija, who has provided me with the atmosphere and environment to conduct my scientific work in the best way possible.

Gratitude and praise be to Allah, and we ask Him for assistance to start a new book and complete what we have begun to fulfill our scientific mission.

Mohamed Kazem Al-Ibrahim Al Mouhajer
Beirut 2022

Preface

The science of economics, with all its data and dimensions, indicates that it is an ethical science, meaning that its purpose targets the human being, leading him to the highest levels of progress in all its material and spiritual dimensions.

Based on this perspective, the science of economics may not be defined solely in terms of maximizing wealth or promoting economic growth, efficiency, economic stability, and so forth. Rather, its effects extend to be a method and tool for social, economic, and cultural reform in a way that it constitutes a lever for humanity and his central position in existence.

For it to be so, it must be based on a vision, concepts, and normative principles characterized by a deep understanding of the phenomena of existence and the interpretation of objectives and goals. Its scope must be broadened to encompass theoretical wisdom, which requires humans to know what they need to know in order to evaluate practical wisdom and the correctness of its approach and procedures. Therefore, it is inevitable that its intersections will be found in other sciences, especially philosophy, as a foundational perspective governing the angle through which economic and social phenomena are examined and understood, thus determining the approach to addressing them and the direction of the required growth and development that leads to the elevation of a human being. It will also find its intersections in other fields such as legal, educational, and ethical realms and so on.

In our current era, the era of globalization and the information revolution, in which liberal thought prevails almost absolutely in most countries of the world, creating with it a type of new human being, like that imposed by liberal economic theory, characterized by imaginary maturity, keen on his individual and personal interest, cautious. And selfish, unable to comprehend the essence of truth, nobility, or human transcendence, as acknowledged in the writings of liberal thinkers.[1] Certainly, this new human being is not the dream of humanity, and Demos's declaration of liberal thought's victory and the "end of history" cannot constitute convincing rational and scientific arguments. Hence rise the motives that prompted us to delve into a thought that constitute today a vital intellectual heritage that moves with the acceleration of history in societies, especially Islamic ones—a thought that plays today a first-class role in the process of achieving ideological visions that preserve psychological and social balances and inspire individual talents, as the thinker Muhammad Arkoun describes it in his book (*History of Arab-Islamic Thought*).

Our intention in undertaking this work was never to propose alternatives that compete with the premises of liberal thought; rather, it was undoubtedly to introduce an economic civilizational thought scientifically aligned with our level of development in the twenty-first century. This thought serves as a reference point for refining the methodologies of our lifestyles and our perspectives related with in a coherent manner rather than a conflicting one.

The most important and prominent question, however, is whether there is a scientifically justified method capable of deriving an Islamic economic thought based on its intellectual and cognitive foundations, especially considering that Islamic thought has not designated a specific domain titled "economics" in its literature. Nevertheless, the aspects it directly addresses, and its comprehensive vision of humanity and the universe, encompass topics such as existential thought, knowledge, ethical systems, worship, transactions, contracts, obligations, rulings, or policies.

Through these topics, directly or indirectly formulated, it establishes general principles, flexible frameworks, and overarching laws, allowing reason and experience alongside divine enlighten-

---

[1] For a comprehensive understanding, refer to *Economics of the Twenty-First Century* by William Hale and Kenneth B. Taylor, translated by Hassan Abdul Allah Badr and Dr. Abdul Wahab Hamid Rashid, distributed by the Center for Arab Unity Studies in Beirut (2009).

ment to flourish. This leads to the development of systems, laws, and advanced theories because Islam fundamentally believes in the laws of evolution in all fields. Therefore, the richness of Islamic humanitarian thought makes it a reference point for deriving a scientific economic thought where reason and experience blend within the context of divine enlightenment, adaptable for application and keeping pace with current significant developments.

This is what prompted us to undertake this work in order to demonstrate this contemporary Islamic political and economic thought, giving our work legitimacy.

For us to adopt the scientific approach with a solid classification and understandable sequence, and in harmony with what we launched at the beginning of this preface, it is necessary to define the contexts of this work according to three approaches that are placed in three parts.

In the first part, we discuss theoretical wisdom and Islam's vision of it (the theory of existence and knowledge; the concept of humans; the concept of the state, freedom, and justice; and the theory of ethics) as basic principles and normative foundations for understanding our economic starting points, thus paving the way for us to try in the second part to define the Islamic economic doctrine with its basic foundations.

As for the third part, we will try, from an Islamic perspective, to address theories in Islamic economics followed by economic policies that constitute a necessity for human advancement according to what Islamic thought holds.

It is essential to emphasize, within the context of our work in the first part, that we are not engaging in a philosophical inquiry into the axes of philosophical doctrines. Rather, we are presenting the theoretical philosophical foundations that influence economics, its formation, and its direction, whether indirectly or directly, as well as the philosophy of economics. This includes some indications of the validity of Islamic thought foundations in this field, along with discussions of other opinions when necessary.

I must note that this research of mine is not a philosophical discussion that requires discussing intellectual currents; rather, it deals with the philosophical aspect that aims to enhance the desired economic vision. There is no escape here from dealing with what philosophical thought has led to from its major thinkers, whether divine Islamic or liberal thinkers and the intellectual conviction that I have generated from them, without elaboration and lengthy connotations.

A final point in this preface must be pointed out before we give subsequent indications of the correctness of its path. Islamic thought will not claim exclusivity in the ruling because reason has the leading position in determining the truth of statements. Even if human beings differ, agree, or differ in their ability and mental perspective, the divine mind and its message are directed to all human beings and not to a specific sect or group. Certainly, the possibility of meeting with other intellectual proposals is something within this context, and we will refer to that whenever necessary.

Part 1

The Philosophical Foundations of Islamic Thought

Chapter 1

Existence and Knowledge

Just a field observation of human behavior shows a clear contrast between behaviors based on the belief in the Creator and His godly message to the created and behaviors of those who deny the divine existence. This appears clearly in economic behavior, especially the consumption pattern that it follows. Hence, it is legitimate to discuss this topic within the context of our book and its implications, which we will discuss further in the second part of this work.

Existence is what exists, even though some speakers and wise men have attempted to define existence. Some indicated that it is "the fixed positive and the negated absolute" or that "existence is that which we can speak about, and nonexistence is that which we cannot speak about," among other interpretations.

Despite this, what closely comes to mind and what is achieved with conviction is the denial of the definition of existence. This is because existence is self-evident as nothing is more knowledgeable than existence and there is no more general meaning than it. Many great thinkers have mentioned this, including the divine scientist, philosopher, and supreme mystic Al-Shirazi, who confirms this in his book *The Supreme Wisdom*: "Existence by itself exists, and all other things besides existence do not exist by themselves, but through accidental existences. In reality, existence is what exists, just as addition is the additive, not what is presented to it of substance, quantity, quality, etc."[2]

As the eminent Allama Nasir al-Din al-Tusi states in his book *The Disclosure of the Intended in Abstracting Belief*, "There is nothing more known than existence, for there is no more comprehensive meaning than it."[3]

To demonstrate the validity of what we have concluded by negating the definition of existence, we find no better authority to return to than the chief sheikh, Abu Ali al-Husayn Ibn Sina, in his book *Metaphysics of the Healing*, where he states: "Existence is the first of concepts, and its definition is impossible. It is the first and foremost in conception." In his commentary on this, he elaborates further:

> As for the first statement, they mentioned two aspects of it.
>
> The first type of knowledge involves understanding that a concept can have both negative and positive aspects. Intuitive primary knowledge and belief are based on perception, so this knowledge is preceded by the perception of existence and nonexistence. What precedes the conception of the primary is that it is primary. We imagine existence as primary intuition.
>
> The second is the human being's knowledge of his existence is not acquired and includes absolute existence, so his knowledge of absolute existence is before knowledge of his existence, and what precedes the primary is more worthy of being primary.
>
> As for the second statement, which is the impossibility of defining existence, if it were pos-

---

2 Sadr al-Din al-Shirazi, *Supreme Wisdom in the Four Journeys* (Al-Mahajjah al-Bayda Publishing House, 2011), 1:41–42.

3 Nasir al-Din Muhammad ibn Hasan al-Tusi, *The Disclosure of the Intended in Abstracting Belief* (Al-Alami Publishing House, 2005), 5.

sible to define it, it would either be defined by itself, by something within it, or by something external to it. The first possibility is invalid, as it implies that something is known before it is known. Similarly, the second possibility, because its parts, whether all or some of them, constitute a single existence, and the individual is a part of nature, also implies the necessity for something to be similar to it, even if it doesn't exist. When these parts come together, either the attribute of existence occurs or it doesn't. If it doesn't, existence would be described as nonexistent matter. If it does occur, then that collective becomes before it—either as an agent or a recipient of the action—thus defining itself becomes a definition of the external, and this is absurd.

As for defining its external necessities, it is also invalid, because unless we know the existence of that necessity and its association with existence, it would not be known to it. The association is also a type of existence because it is the existence of the description of something, which necessitates defining the absolute by the restricted and defining existence by existence.

As for the third statement (which is that existence is the foremost in conception, and that is because it is the most knowledgeable of things. Our knowledge of everything is an expression of occurrence to us, and within it is the absolute attainment, so the absolute occurrence is more primal and more known than the occurrence of this or that, occurrence is synonymous with existence, and this is an intuitive matter)...[4]

[4] Mulla Sadra, commentary and annotation on *The Metaphysics of the Healing*, by Ibn Sina (Arab History Institute, 2007), 1:112–114.

From this, we conclude that existence, insofar as it exists, is only known by existence, so how can existence be known by it?

In defining existence, the wise pointed out the compatibility of existence with entity.

Al-Tusi has pointed out the continuity of existence and entity and their inseparability to the point that everything in general exists absolutely, and everything that does not exist is nonexistent and is nothing.[5] Here it is necessary to point to mental existence to avoid confusion as the main sheikh Ibn Sina refers to everything that is an entity in essence or conception.

So everything that does not exist in objects is nothing in objects. However, it is a thing in terms of its intelligibility, as it exists in the mind in this regard… Absolute existence without condition equals absolute entity without limitation. The mental corresponds to the mental, and the physical corresponds to the physical.[6]

The first thing that comes to the human mind is the question of how existence exists, which is the main question in philosophy, along with the question of the immortality of the soul and freedom of will, where there are abundant debates about the existence or nonexistence of a Creator and the justification for existence through nature. However, I will not present the opinions of philosophers and thinkers who have been divided between affirming or denying the existence of God, despite the importance of opinions, as stated by Saint Anselm and René Descartes regarding their proof of the existence of the Creator, as well as the materialists and some positivists in denying divine existence, but what is necessary is to present the methodology of proving the existence of the Creator as stated by the philosophers and sages of Islam, and settled in our mind due to our need to consolidate our ideas that will appear in the field of economic thought that we will discuss.

The universe, with all its dimensions containing everything from the largest to the smallest, has been proven by modern science

---

5 Nasir al-Din Muhammad ibn Hasan al-Tusi, *The Disclosure of the Intended in Abstracting Belief*, 15.

6 Ibn Sina, *The Metaphysics of the Healing*, 119.

through scientific experiments to be formed through what are called quarks and neutrinos, which constitute the basic building blocks of atoms such as hydrogen and nitrogen, and from which the entire material world is formed, starting from microscopic entities like amoebas to large mammals. Within this universe, there are mountains, oceans, and forests with endless diversity. Even the Earth itself is just a planet in a solar system, and the planets within it are of immense sizes beyond imagination. Our solar system is merely a small corner of the universe, a cradle of time and space, vast and expansive, difficult to comprehend its secrets.[7]

And thanks to the growth of knowledge in the physical sciences, our understanding of the secrets of this universe expands, I would like to point out strongly, is that science has revealed regarding the matter that constitutes things, as the world of matter is in continuous development and renewal, and the occurrence of the world according to that was an inevitable result of its renewable nature, which confirms this scientific proof beyond doubt that the universe was created.

Before discussing the existence of Allah Almighty as described by religious scholars, it's important to clarify the concepts of obligation, possibility, and abstention. The concept of existence and things in general predates the necessary and the non-necessary. If the necessary is associated with existence, it becomes an obligation; if associated with nonexistence, it becomes an abstention. When the non-necessary is associated with either one or both, it leads to general and specific possibilities.[8]

Based on what has been presented, if the world is contingent, as we have indicated, then it must have a cause, which is a necessity. And if the possible becomes necessary, it becomes obligatory for existence, and this is what is required. Here, we say that the cause is ancient, and the ancient implies necessity.

In this context, Ibn Sina adds that the necessary existence in itself has no cause, and among its attributes is that it is necessarily

---

[7] Julian Baggini, *Philosophy: Key Themes* (Al Takwin Publishing House, 2010), 141–142.

[8] Sadr al-Din al-Shirazi, *Supreme Wisdom in the Four Journeys*, 1:70.

obligatory from every aspect, with no equivalent to it, no participant in its reality,[9] and so forth, its attributes of divine essence with perfection, power, and knowledge... It is worth noting that some Western thinkers, in their proof of the existence of Allah, argue that it is necessary existence, as indicated by a method different from what the thinker René Descartes has mentioned.

Based on what has been stated, existence is created by the action of Allah God Almighty and is an obligatory existence as He is the Creator of nonbeing into being, and the world in its current existence, the things that exist are either things whose existence is not by our choice or things whose existence is by our choice and action, and the approach of knowledge in the first aspect has been referred to by the wise as "theoretical wisdom," and knowledge of matters in the second aspect has been called "practical wisdom." Theoretical philosophy (or theoretical wisdom) aims to complete the self by knowing, whereas practical philosophy (or practical wisdom) aims to complete the self not only by knowing but also by knowing what to do and acting upon it. The goal of theoretical philosophy is to believe in an opinion, while the goal of practical philosophy is to know an opinion that is in action.[10]

As for the methodology of the relationship between them and their mutual effects, it is in the context of our work that is presented. There are intellectual propositions regarding the topic of existence that must be mentioned due to their relevance to the course of the research.

Essence and accident

Possible existence can either have its existence unassociated with a subject, which is called "essence," or it can be associated with a subject, which is called "accident." By *subject*, we mean the object that is constituted by itself, the constituent of what takes place in it. The object is either constituted by the state, or the state is qualified for

9 Ibn Sina, *The Metaphysics of the Healing*, 1:145.

10 Ibid., 1:6.

it since one must need the other. The first is called matter, and the second is called subject. And the state in the first is called form, and in the second, it is called accident. The subject and matter share the same relation as two specifics under one general thing, which is the subject, and the form and the incident share the same as two specifics under one general thing, which is the situation. The subject is more specific than the object, and the nonspecific is more general than the general nonexistence. Everything that is not in a place is not in a subject and is not reflected, and for this reason, it is permissible for some substance to be present in something else. Since the definition of accident includes an evidentiary restriction, it is presented in the division of essence.[11]

In a different expression, Sheikh al-Rais Ibn Sina elaborates, "The existent without being inherent in any of the things with this characteristic is not in the subject at all, so it is called essence. The existent in another thing, that another thing has the essence and the type in itself, not as a part of it, and without its separation from that thing. This means that its existence in itself is its existence for that thing. This is what is called 'accident,' and it is existent in the subject."[12]

Existent by essence and existent by accident. An existent either has an independent occurrence in objects, so it exists by itself, whether it is an essence or an accident. Even though the accident does not exist except in its place, it exists in reality. The existence of the accident is not the same as the existence of its subject, as the subject may exist without the accident, then the accident exists in it, like the body when darkness settles in it after it was absent.

However, if the existent does not have an independent occurrence in objects, then it exists by accident, including mental legal matters that cannot be achieved in objects, then it is said that they exist in objects by accident.[13]

---

[11] Nasir al-Din Muhammad ibn Hasan al-Tusi, *The Disclosure of the Intended in Abstracting Belief*, 118.

[12] Ibn Sina, *The Metaphysics of the Healing*, 1:209.

[13] Nasir al-Din Muhammad ibn Hasan al-Tusi, *The Disclosure of the Intended in Abstracting Belief*, 57.

In the context of existence, in essence itself, we say "so-and-so is a human being," which is to be confirmed and identical with its predicate on something that is the same subject and its existence in itself. As for the context of what is present in the accident, you say "one is a lawyer," which means that his credibility and the correspondence of his predicate are not the same subject and its existence in itself but, rather, with something else that compares it or performs it.

Force and act

The concept of force falls under every characteristic or state of something that affects others, whether it is essence or accident and whether it has a will or not, such as heat, a "force" that affects others, and forced movements caused by nature, for example. Force is something that has the power to do something that has force. For instance, when we say "the white cloth is potentially black," we mean it can turn black, and power in this context means possibility since it has the ability in general to act and not to act if it is a force to act and the possibility of it being reacted and not. Thus, something whose existence is possible is termed "potentially existent," while the possibility of acceptance of the recipient and its reaction is termed "reactive force," and the occurrence of that action is termed "act."

The main sheikh Ibn Sina adds to this that the ratio of action to force is the ratio of completeness to imperfection. Since the first subject of the name force is an action in reality, here, when they named possibility "force," they named the related matter, which is occurrence and existence, "act" because the comparison of what was initially termed "act" to what is now termed "force" is similar to the comparison of what is now termed "act" to the previously termed "force." In this comparison, they named occurrence "act," whether it is an action, reaction, or otherwise.

This possibility is the potential force, and it only exists when there is a deficiency in ability or effectiveness, for the agent may be lacking in effectiveness, needing authority, habit, or tool to become effective, just as the recipient may be deficient in ability and far from a readiness for acceptance, lacking prerequisites to become truly capable of action.[14]

Cause and effect

The issuance of something resulting from something else, the emerging is an effect and the issuing is a cause, whether the issuance is by way of independence, as in the case of a complete cause, or as an attachment a part of the cause. The part of the cause is something from which another command issues, but not by way of independence, for it is within the definition. The sections of the cause are divided between efficiency, materiality, formality, and finality. The cause is what a thing needs, and it is either part of the effect or external to it. The first is either a part by which the thing occurs by action or by force. The first is form, and the second is matter. If it is external, it is either influential or the effect stops on it. The first is an actor, and the second is an end.[15]

A basic and important indication that is necessary relates to the impossibility of chaining causes in one chain without end because each one of them is impossible to obtain without an obligatory cause. But what is necessary is also due to what is impossible, so there must be a cause in and of itself that is a party to the chain.

Knowledge (epistemology)

The soul's inclination toward perfection will only occur through knowledge. It is an absolute truth that does not require proof but raises several questions about what we know. What should we know? How can we know? It requires certainty—that is, not just a belief that can be true or false but rather reaching certainty in knowledge. In other words, reaching the truth. Based on this, the results of the subject of knowledge are not limited to a branch of the sciences

[14] Ibn Sina, *The Metaphysics of the Healing*, 2:731.

[15] Nasir al-Din Muhammad ibn Hasan al-Tusi, *The Disclosure of the Intended in Abstracting Belief*, 97.

required by the contexts of our lives but rather include the comprehensive body of sciences, especially the human ones (economics, law, society, etc.).

In this context, philosophers and thinkers have focused on theories and doctrines regarding their views on the ways to attain knowledge (rationalists, empiricists, realists, idealists, foundationalists, pragmatists, skeptics, phenomenologists) and have elaborated on their theories and arguments, which undoubtedly serve as enlightenment for the human mind, whether one agrees with some or none or refutes the truth of their conclusions. Nevertheless, you can't help but appreciate the intellectual contribution they have made.

In this study, it is not for us to discuss each perspective and its conclusions, but those looking for a comprehensive vision should return to the large amount of literature available, ancient and modern, in this field.[16]

As for the subject of our study, we will limit ourselves to the important doctrines that constitute a presence in our contemporary world.

These doctrines not only shape our lifestyles but also undoubtedly have a significant impact on the subject of our study: political economy. Therefore, we will focus on presenting the rational and empirical doctrines with some exploration into Islamic thought on the "theory of knowledge."

Rationalism

This is what several Western philosophers have taken, as we will explain. Islamic philosophy can also be referred to as rationalism with varying methodologies, as we will also explain. But before presenting the rationalist doctrine, it is necessary to point out the background of what the rational thinkers went to, which is presented in Greek thought and as the divine Sadr al-Din al-Shirazi referred to it in his

---

[16] Look for example:
- Julian Baggini, *Philosophy: Key Themes* (Al Takwin Publishing House, 2010).
- Muhammad Baqir al-Sadr, *Our Philosophy* (Al Taarof publishing house, 1982).

travels, as well as al-Fakhr al-Razi in his Oriental Investigations, and it is centered on the idea that "what the soul attains of knowledge is inherent within it, existing in it from the beginning of its existence," which refers to Socrates and some Greek thinkers who said that the human soul is ancient. That sciences existed in the soul from the beginning of its existence, which is what is meant by its subjectivity. Effort and striving for knowledge and knowledge are the only ways to lift the drawn veil, and for this reason, they said this: The teacher does not create knowledge in the learner but rather works to remove the membrane and veil that covers knowledge and prevents it from emerging, and thus he has brought out that knowledge hidden within oneself.[17]

After this indication that we have provided, we believe that it contains something suggestive for philosophers of the seventeenth and eighteenth centuries AD (such as Descartes, Leibniz, and Spinoza) and perhaps for philosophers who preceded this era. The means of acquiring knowledge, according to rationalists, must rely on reason. Here, thinking does not depend on experience but rather starts from inherent basic truths within the self that have not come through trial and experience. These are priori ideas.

Since the priori ideas of the rationalists are intuitive and necessary, meaning they do not require one to acquire or contemplate as a concept the notion of existence and that the whole is greater than the part, and the event does not exist without a cause, these are matters that do not require proof of their validity. Rationalists believe that this fundamental pre-experiential knowledge enables them to proceed in thinking without resorting to experience. Therefore, obtaining subsequent theoretical knowledge must be by the priori information and knowledge, through reasoning and deduction.

Based on this context, rationalists assert the principle of causality, stating that all knowledge arises from previous knowledge and thus progresses in sequence until it culminates in primary intellectual

[17] Muhammad Hussein al-Tabatabaei, *Explanation of the End of Wisdom* (Arab History Institute, 2015), 2:204–205.

knowledge. For this reason, prior knowledge is considered the initial cause of knowledge.

The scientific duty necessitates, under the title of rationalism, referring to the eminent thinker and philosopher Immanuel Kant (1724–1804), whom many thinkers described as "a mountain of profound thought" and who presented, through his works (particularly *Critique of Pure Reason*, *Critique of Practical Reason*, and *Critique of Judgment*), a deep and advanced theory in epistemology that remains an important intellectual reference in our contemporary history, whether one believes in its propositions, remains undecided, or criticizes its content. Regardless of one's stance, one cannot help but admire, appreciate, and be grateful for what Kant has contributed to humanity's intellectual heritage. In the context of our study, it is necessary to mention, even briefly, some of his ideas on epistemology.

If we are allowed to summarize Kant's views on knowledge, despite the reservations about being concise, which may overlook many aspects, nuances, or even detailed foundations that may not seem necessary to us despite their importance, then we must acknowledge and apologize for this audacity in attempting to condense as presented here.

Kant asserts that our knowledge begins with experience, through subjects that affect our senses and lead to the formation of representations, thus engaging our understanding. Therefore, the origin of human knowledge derives from a common root, as Kant puts it—namely, sensibility and understanding. Sensibility provides us with the subjects while understanding allows us to vary them. However, in the human mind, there exists knowledge independent of experience and even sensory impressions. Kant refers to this knowledge as "a priori," distinguishing it from empirical knowledge derived afterward—that is, knowledge sourced from experience. In a priori knowledge, every judgment entails its necessity, thus becoming a priori judgment.[18]

---

[18] Immanuel Kant, *Critique of Pure Reason* (Arab Translation Organization, 2013), 84.

So intuition and concepts constitute the two elements of all our knowledge, whereby there are no concepts without intuition to match them, nor intuition without concepts that can give us knowledge. These two elements are either pure or experimental: experimental when sensation is involved in them and pure when representation is not mixed with any sensation. Therefore, pure intuition contains only the image by which something is perceived, and pure concepts contain only the thought image of a subject in general. Pure intuitions or concepts alone are possible a priori, while experience is only possible a posteriori.

Thus, without sensibility, no object will be given to us, and without understanding, no object will be thought of. Ideas without content are empty, and intuitions without concepts are blind. Understanding cannot perceive anything, and the senses cannot think of anything. It is only through their union that knowledge can arise.[19]

On the other hand, Kant asserts that there is relevant knowledge that goes beyond the field of all possible experiences and resorts to concepts for which experience, wherever it may be, is unable to provide a corresponding subject. It suggests that it extends the range of our judgments beyond all limits of experience.

This is knowledge far superior to everything that understanding can learn in the field of phenomena, and it falls upon pure reason and contemplation not to exceed them. They are the existence of God, freedom of the will, and the immortality of the soul.

Kant's creativity also shines in practical applied knowledge. Through his work *Groundwork of the Metaphysics of Morals*, he highlights his profound thought in its most beautiful manifestations, crafting a framework for human behavior based on theoretical reason.

Empiricism

Empiricist philosophers fundamentally reject the notion that the mind contains certain ideas and concepts from birth. They have

---

[19] Ibid., 125–126.

opposed rationalism, and here we refer to some of their most important philosophers, such as Locke, Berkeley, and Hume, who were contemporaries in a historical period almost parallel to their rationalist predecessors.

John Locke, in his work *An Essay Concerning Human Understanding* (1690), rejects the theory that the mind contains certain ideas and concepts from birth. Although we need initial ideas to be able to think, the mind is, from birth, a blank slate, and it acquires ideas through experience via our five senses.[20]

Therefore, empiricists generally do not acknowledge innate knowledge and confine human thought and the means of acquiring knowledge within the bounds of the empirical field, considering it the source of all knowledge. They move from the particular to the general in their judgments, rejecting any theoretical wisdom based on contemplation and abstract thinking divorced from experience.

Materialist philosophy and positivist philosophy fall under the doctrine of the empiricists, which are still present in our contemporary history. (The most prominent materialists are the Marxist school, and positivist philosophy is considered a cornerstone of contemporary liberal thought.)

Here are some additional lines regarding existentialist philosophy and its derivatives, particularly logical positivism. Existentialist philosophy negates any issue unless its meaning is grounded in sensory and empirical evidence subject to experimentation. Consequently, it condemns scientific matters that do not stem from sensory data but rather express laws inferred from sensory evidence.[21]

As for logical positivism from the Austrian school in the eighteenth century, Wittgenstein and others to Professor Ayer, who is considered the imam of logical positivism in modern history, their opinion is limited to the fact that positivism indicates the meaning whose rightness or wrongness can be verified within the limits of sensory experience. Any issue lacking sensory meaning or empirical existence becomes meaningless mere linguistic constructs.

---

[20] Julian Baggini, *Philosophy*, 35.

[21] Muhammad Baqir al-Sadr, *Our Philosophy*, 87.

Therefore, the issue of contemplation and theoretical wisdom is nothing but nonsense. If you say God is the Eternal All-Powerful Knower whose validity cannot be tested sensibly or experimentally, then it is just nonsense.

Knowledge in Islamic thought

In providing us with knowledge according to the contexts of Islamic thought, we start from the created existence as we have previously indicated. This existence is created by the Almighty, which is a factual reality that does not require evidence or definition. The Creator has created a divine cosmic system characterized by the comprehensiveness of the universe, and it transitions indeed to the higher celestial realm.

At the center of this system are human beings, created in the best of forms, distinguished from all other creatures by their intellect. This distinguished creature, in its journey toward knowledge and learning, was not left by the Almighty without means to attain knowledge. Rather, two sources grant him knowledge based on his effort and varying psychological readiness. First, through transmission, revelation via prophets, and second, through reason and what it can comprehend. These are complementary sources, not contradictory. We will address the second of these sources and their significance through the studies of philosophers and Islamic thinkers, thereby proving the divine mission of the prophets and the scope of necessary knowledge they conveyed.

In our understanding of how the mind acquires knowledge, our knowledge of the external world is divided into two categories. It can either be acquired through mental representation, where the object is present in the mind in the form of a mental image (acquired knowledge), or without the mediation of mental representation, where the object exists independently (presentational knowledge). Acquired knowledge is conceptual and intellectual, necessitated by the mind, derived from presentational knowledge. It is an ideal or mental existence, present in its external reality to the perceiver even if perceived from afar.[22]

To elucidate rationality and the acquisition of knowledge, Muslim philosophers referred to four levels of reason:

1. *The potential reason.* This level represents the state where the soul is devoid of all intelligible.
2. *The reason by acquisition.* This level entails the rationalization of self-evident truths through conceptualization and acceptance.
3. *The reason by actualization.* This level involves rationalizing theories.
4. *The derived reason.* At this level, one rationalizes all acquired intelligible, whether self-evident or theoretical, corresponding to the realities of the celestial or terrestrial worlds, without material occupation.[23]

It's worth noting here that Aristotle divided action into three categories: the potential reason, the actual reason, and the active reason. The philosopher Al-Farabi added a fourth category, which is the derived reason.

The division changed, as seen in the doctrine of transcendent theosophy by the Shirazi mystics, who omitted the active reason and added the reason by sovereignty.

The division was as mentioned above, with the level of the material reason, like the mind of a child devoid of all forms but ready to receive and comprehend them.

The second stage is the stage of rationalizing intuitive truths, the third stage is the stage of rationalizing theories, and the final stage is the presence of all rationalizations for the soul without omitting anything, which is the derived reason.[24]

---

[22] For more information, see the following:

- Muhammad Hussein al-Tabatabaei, *Explanation of the End of Wisdom.*
- Sadr al-Din al-Shirazi, *Supreme Wisdom in the Four Journeys.*

[23] Muhammad Hussein al-Tabatabaei, *Explanation of the End of Wisdom*, 353.

[24] Ibid., 353–354.

Understanding the mental images of material existence and how to emanate these images, Muslim thinkers believe that there must be an outlet for these images. Either the soul does them and accepts them, or it is something outside the material or abstract, and they—Muslim thinkers—see that the fact of the soul is the one that overflows them and acts upon them. It is impossible since one thing must be both active and capable, and it is false. As for the fact that the emanating thing is a material matter, it is also false since the material is weaker in existence than the abstract, so it cannot be its agent, and the agent is stronger in existence than the reason. Therefore, they believe that the emanating form of mental images is an abstract, rational essence separate from matter, with which the soul that is prepared for reason is united to the same extent. Her preparation and the mental images she formulates will overflow from it.[25]

However, the actual images are mental images devoid of positive and negative, and here is the second level (the reason by acquisition), which is aware of the images and involves the belief judgment for the sake of objective knowledge.

Here, it is essential to clarify that mental images carry within their knowledge that is either innate (a priori), which does not require acquisition or reflection and is called necessary, meaning it doesn't require any mental effort from the individual to acquire it. This type of knowledge falls into two categories: conceptual (such as the concept of existence, and all concepts cannot be acquired through evidence because they lack gender or action) or intuitive (such as believing that the whole is greater than the part). The other category is theoretical, which requires acquisition, reflection, and thought. This is where the stage of "the reason in act" comes into play.

These perceived images acquired by the reason fall into two categories:

1) *Material images.* These images are based on material existence, such as matter, position, and place. Such images cannot be considered intellectually actual according to this

[25] Muhammad Hussein al-Tabatabaei, *Explanation of the End of Wisdom*, 355–356.

material existence, nor can they be sensed except through presentation (propositions) like quantity, quality, relation, place, time, situation, ownership, action, and reaction.[26]

2) *Abstract images.* These are images abstracted from materiality, position, and place. The intellectually actual image derived from something abstracted from materiality is always intellectually actual, whether its reason is external or not.[27] This is where the derived intellect comes into play, influencing contemplation, transcendent wisdom, and the realities of the celestial or terrestrial world.

Knowledge through divine revelation

Some Western philosophers who believe in the existence of God (including Descartes and Spinoza) have denied the divine mission as there is no need for messengers as long as God has created rational humans, capable with their minds to perceive all the laws of nature without the need for revelation. Thus, they denied any knowledge that could come to us from God Almighty.

We have previously discussed that according to Islamic thought, Allah has created a comprehensive divine cosmic system that extends through its phases to the higher world, with the highest stage marked by death and the transition of the soul from the lower world. Thus, if the outcomes of the initial phases in the lower world determine the position of the soul in the higher world, then the existence of divine missions becomes at least necessary as an argument for informing about renewing the human's position in the higher world and legitimizing punishment and reward. This necessity is imposed by the divine cosmic system. In the world of existence, divine enlightenment is indispensable as a renewing path for human worldly behavior as it supports reason in its judgments and derives rulings where reason does not suffice, such as in religious laws. With divine enlightenment, knowledge of good and evil, which reason alone cannot

[26] Nasir al-Din al-Tusi, *Abstract of Beliefs*, 181–252.

[27] Sadr al-Din al-Shirazi, *Supreme Wisdom*, part 3, 1:736–737.

discern, is obtained, among other things. This makes the path of human life toward perfection through divine enlightenment easier, more knowledgeable, and farther away from the evils resulting from human relationships and their relationship with nature.

The reason, which has been allocated a significant importance in Islamic thought as a source of knowledge, should never contradict or conflict with what is established by religious teachings. The relationship between reason and revelation is complementary, negating any contradiction. Its purpose is to expand knowledge of the divine cosmic system and establish behavioral guidelines for practical human intellect. In this context, we can cite a passage from the Muslim Arab philosopher Ibn Rushd:

> If this Sharia law is true and calls for reasoning that leads to knowledge of the truth, then we, Muslims, know with certainty that rational inquiry does not contradict what the law has stated. For truth does not contradict truth, but rather affirms and testifies to it.
>
> If this is the case, then if rational inquiry leads to knowledge of something existing, this existence inevitably is either something the law has been silent about or something it has acknowledged.
>
> If a matter has not been explicitly addressed by the law, a jurist can deduce it through legal analogy. If the Sharia has already addressed it, the apparent meaning of its pronouncement may align with reasoning or contradict it. If there is alignment, there is no contention. If there is a contradiction, interpretation is needed.[28]

[28] Abu al-Walid ibn Rushd, *The Distinction between Wisdom and Shariah from Communication* (Al-Maarif Publishing House, 1983), 31–32.

Therefore, the comprehensive source of knowledge in conjunction with reason is nothing but "divine enlightenment," encompassing its data in Islamic thought: existence, value system, worship, transactions, and injunctions, which include obligations and policies.

These are the topics of wisdom for human reason as well as the path of human behavior in building the universe.

This path is indicated by the verses of the Holy Quran: "Just as We have sent among you a messenger from yourselves reciting to you Our verses and purifying you and teaching you the Book and wisdom and teaching you that which you did not know."[29]

[29] Surah Al-Baquarah, verse 151.

Chapter 2

The Concept of the Human Being

In the context provided, we mentioned the chapter "The Concept of the Human Being" as a separate section from the concept of freedom. It may create ambiguity since it is difficult to separate these concepts independently. Rather, we decided to present the discussion on freedom before delving into the segment on humanity for methodological purposes, aiming to provide clear and more coherent insights that align with concepts of existence and essence. Therefore, we will directly address the topic of freedom in the following segment, intending to encompass the concepts smoothly.

On the other hand, our presentation of the concept of the human will certainly does not limit itself to superficial sensory perception. Instead, it falls within theoretical wisdom concerning what we ought to know. Therefore, its relevance extends to worldly studies such as economics, which falls under practical wisdom.

The context of thought that we follow requires us to understand the human being in his spiritual dimensions in addition to the tangible material. The intellectual state constitutes the existential cause for the formation of the will, and practical wisdom determines the possibility and methods for bringing about economic action, as in this work of ours, and thus the necessities of determining the axis of the processes of cause and effect in the sense of creation. Voluntary based on the theoretical perspective to understand reality more deeply and certainly the depth of its causality. Therefore, we need to delve into the "concept of the human" in search for "truth" in its practical material reality.

This approach constitutes the philosophy of economics, which is necessary for logical and intellectual understanding when interpreting economic phenomena about humans. This approach necessarily leads us to answers that have preoccupied global thought and still do—answers that give a clear intellectual vision of what the thinker Immanuel Kant proposed:

- What can I know?
- What should I do?
- What can I hope for?

These three issues are summed up in one question: "What is a human being?"

Certainly, humanity, in its quest for truth, cannot be satisfied with what the senses present to it regarding existence and the universe. Human beings, endowed with reason, strive in every time and place to assert their right to knowledge not only as material beings but also as spiritual or intellectual entities. This spiritual and material dimension necessarily leads humanity to explore its existence within the dialectic of "God, man, nature," which has been a crucial axis in human thought. Its contemporary presence in the twenty-first century continues to cast its shadows, not only as a philosophical vision confined within belief systems but also reflected in human behavior and the formulation of policies, especially economic and social policies. In our current reality, liberal ideology dominates economic policies in most countries worldwide, declaring its triumph. The policies are often treated as indisputable principles governing many political systems and their relations. Intellectual vision forms the fundamental reference for this ideological tendency and liberal policies. Therefore, we cannot evade the necessity of examining and discussing the intellectual aspect of this dialectic, particularly within liberal perspectives. We should consider Western thinkers who have left significant imprints on this contemporary reality, followed by an Islamic perspective to clarify the position of humans within this dialectic under investigation.

For several centuries, specifically from the fifteenth century until our present era, Western intellectual tendencies have intertwined and clashed in their perspectives on the divine existence, making it difficult to establish meaningful generalizations without contradicting many similar cases that point to another direction. We notably observe the negative tendency in refuting the Christian theological thought of God's existence. In very few instances, there is a refutation of the Jewish Christian divine theology and its claims of supernatural origin or the use of authority in religious and moral matters. Thus, we have not witnessed the existence of a stable opinion regarding the evidence or the precise relationship between rational inference, scientific discoveries, and human emotional life. In other words, Western thought is confined to the refutation of the Christian theological God, departing from reaction rather than initiating a separation that takes on the meaning of the absolute in the matter of divine existence and its relationship with humans and nature and according to any method that presents evidence and gives significance, whether rational inference, empirical scientific existence, or introspection of human emotional life. Therefore, what we present here only serves as explanatory signs of fundamental tendencies and the best Western thinkers who have addressed this issue, ultimately leading to clear elucidation of the background of Western thought in its perspective on the phenomena of existence.

Temporal political authority gains its legitimacy from its continued support for the life of the Lord, as Pope Gelasius I (AD 494) wrote, declaring the rule of this world according to the sacred authority of the monks as opposed to the monarchy system on the other hand, where the monks' advantage will prevail. The church, as a religious institution, serves as a reference for solutions, representing the body of God in this world. The Pope is considered the sole reference for solutions, and this is the basis of his infallibility. The church acts as the mediator between the Creator and the creatures.

This trend is accompanied by flagrant phenomena of corruption among the men of the church and resistance to scientific progress. This has posed a challenge to legitimacy and dynamism, sparking intense debates that have defined the dimensions of the church's authority and its reference point. These debates have evolved within intellectual schools and movements (naturalists, empiricists, theologians, atheists, existentialists, etc.) and have continued into our contemporary era. Within the scope of our study, we will present some of the most prominent of these as intellectual currents and thinkers in their perspectives on divine existence and its reflection on the cosmic reference of humanity or nature.

The beginnings were from church thinkers and clerics who laid the foundation to depart from ecclesiastical theology with its faith-based nature toward rational proof of divine existence. Here, we refer, first, to Cardinal Nicholas of Cosa (1401–1464) as one of the prominent figures of the church and a man with a humanitarian inclination, as well as a philosopher and a man of reason. In his writings, he indicates that the fully sacred God is unknown to us, according to Christian theology, which inspires the natural human intellectual ambition to seek real knowledge about God and finite things. The outcome leads toward a contemplative direction, even if the infinite truth remains unattainable. If we cannot penetrate the secret of the infinite God, perhaps we can approach Him diligently and systematically as much as our cognitive tools allow. The divine reason is a formative force creating actual beings in its existence, while the human reason is a conforming force representing the similarity of actual beings. Through abstraction, generalization, and inference, the human mind constructs a world of subjects and organizes similarities rationally. In doing so, the human mind not only fulfills its nature but also approaches closer to the divine model and grasps the mind of God, which is incomprehensible.[30]

An even more extreme position comes from the churchman Giordano Bruno (1548–1600), a Dominican monk who renounced his monastic vows and departed from the Catholic Church.

---

[30] James Collins, *God in Modern Philosophy* (Cultural Diversity House, 2019), 14–27.

Bruno's departure from the Christian faith was not just a passing incident but rather a decisive factor in the formation of his philosophy about God. He refused to accept divine revelation as truth, whether in its Catholic or Protestant form, and he also refused to look at Christian ethics as a path to human happiness. Revelation is treated as hostile to reason and philosophy, and Bruno's philosophy exposes God as the principle and the cause: "Insofar as He is nature itself, or insofar as He appears to us within the scope of this nature and its folds, God and essential nature are one thing, and the only manifestation permitted for this God is natural manifestation." Bruno asserts that there is no realistic, essential transcendence of God over perceptible nature, but there is an endless progress of human intelligence and love toward the infinite essence of nature itself.[31]

The beginnings paved the way for the currents in their perspectives on God to emerge in various directions, which we highlight as follows:

1. Deism or divine rationalism (God without revelation)

A perspective that sees the world as created (i.e., contingent, by one God). This can be perceived through reason alone and contemplation of nature, which reflects the will and power of the Creator God. Therefore, there is no justification for revelation or any intervention if the laws of nature are parallel to God, meaning it is an inclination toward asserting the universe's unity. Human reason is sufficient to comprehend the laws of nature without the need for revelation.

And what is faith in the unseen and revelation other than myths? The Creator's task ended with the creation of the universe, and He has no concern with intervening in the affairs of the universe. Therefore, He is excluded from any cognitive process, which has become rational and sensory. Under this rational view, rationalists, empiricists, and positivists converge…albeit with divergent methodologies. However, they all agree on the existence of a God

[31] Ibid., 40–53.

devoid of revelation, thus stripping religion of its sanctity. Here, it is necessary to briefly review some of the most prominent thinkers of these currents.

The rationalists, most notably Descartes, Spinoza, Leibniz, and René Descartes (1596–1650) in his view of the functional use of God. The main task of metaphysics is to establish the first principles of deduction on effective rational foundations to establish a complete system of initially derived facts. God is the rational principle of the deductive system, and without God, there will be no certainty. Thus, he establishes a close connection between the cogito and the reality of the existing God:

> The certainty and truth of all knowledge depends only on knowing the true God, such that before I know Him, I cannot fully know anything else, and the certainty of all other things depends on this, to the point that without this knowledge, we can't know anything else a complete knowledge.[32]

Descartes ends by indicating that God's infinite power is nature.

Benedict Spinoza (1632–1677), who is said to have started where Descartes left off, was greatly influenced by the ideas of Giordano Bruno (whom we mentioned earlier).[33] If we were to summarize Spinoza's view on God in a few lines, we would say that he pointed to the infinite solid power of God as nature perceived by human reason. In his philosophical doctrine, there is no room for the possibility of revelation having any significance, and sacred texts are not sources of theoretical truth:

> I embrace an opinion concerning God and nature that differs entirely from the view

[32] Lafleur, (Meditations on First Philosophy [58–59]), from the previous source, 108.

[33] Abdul-Wahab al-Masiri, *Partial and Comprehensive Secularism* (Al-Shorouq Publishing House, 2002), 2:54.

> defended by modern Christians. I believe that God is, as they say, the immanent cause of all things, but I do not believe that God is a transcendent cause... And I say that many of the attributes which they consider, and all whom I know at least consider, as attributes of God, I see as created things. On the other hand, the things that they consider as created, because of their distinctions, I see as attributes of God, but they misinterpret them. Likewise, I cannot separate God from nature, and this is what everyone I know has done.[34]

Within this context, it is necessary to point out the most prominent thinker, Immanuel Kant, as well as Hegel, among the divine thinkers. But can they be classified among the rationalists? According to Kant, and within certain limits, yes, we can talk about him under the classification of rationalists. As for Hegel, we can perhaps find a relationship with mentalists in various forms.

In this context, Immanuel Kant (1724–1804) emerged at a later stage than the thinkers we have mentioned. The timing of his life allowed him broader exposure as he was a philosopher of the Enlightenment era. His extensive reading of his predecessors' works and his meticulous study, combined with his fervent reason, gave significance to his approach to the rational methodical doctrine of the nature of God. His three major works—*Critique of Pure Reason*, *Critique of Practical Reason*, and *Metaphysics of Morals*—offer the most comprehensive and profound analysis of reason, God, and existence. Kant emerges as a towering figure described as a mountain of thought. Through his works and in brief lines, of course, we do not deny his right at all. But one of the necessities of the context for this study is the subject of the existence of God and his relationship with man and nature so that we can arrive at the furthest judgment of Western thinkers regarding the extent of their influence on the

[34] · Adam Tanner, Works on James Collins, *God in Modern Philosophy*, 117–118.

intellectual state and its practical impact in our contemporary reality in the twenty-first century and in the field of economics specifically.

We must necessarily summarize and always recommend returning to Kant in the field of deeper thought of Western thinkers. First, we must emphasize that Kant had complete personal conviction in the transcendent reality of God, and he did not deviate from this belief throughout his life, which he devoted to deep philosophical contemplation, but linked this belief to the fact that it stems from moral importance as he considers that God is one. Moral postulates, even if at the same time he denied any normative influence as a basis and motivation for moral action—that is, he gave this divine existence a "moral function" based on three main issues: God himself does not serve any methodological purpose in theoretical philosophy, the idea of God leads a function in this section of philosophy, but about existing things, and in ethics, the moral manifestations of the existence of God perform a necessary hypothetical function, not as a source of obligation but rather as means of clarifying some of the results of moral obligation. And in his proof of the existence of God, Kant presents the possible approach in the following way:

> There are two beginnings for proof: the rational conception of the pure possible and the experimental conception of the existing, and each of these two beginnings provides us with two foundations for proof. In the first proof, the rational conception of the possible is taken as a basis, from which we derive the existence of God as a result. The second proof begins with the possible as a given result, and then we return to God describing Him as a necessary cause. The third proof starts from what exists in experience to lead us to an independent first cause, and by analyzing this concept, we deduce the attributes of God. As for the final proof, it begins in the same way, but it ascends directly to the existence of God and His attributes together—and accord-

> ingly, Kant believes—that the first and the third foundations are invalid, and the fourth basis has limited value, and the second proof alone is the true proof.[35]

As for Georges Wilhelm Friedrich Hegel (1770–1831), it is clear from the period of his life that he was after the Age of Enlightenment, which also allowed him to become acquainted with the intense intellectual visions of the seventeenth and eighteenth centuries and the Age of Enlightenment. The German idealism to which he was approaching did not make him possess an independent basis for his philosophical doctrine until after he formulated his theory of the Absolute as a spirit. Hegel's philosophy describes the process in which the spirit immerses itself in the form of nature alien to itself, which then returns to itself in humanity through history.[36]

Therefore, it is apparent that this absolute spirit is different from the God of Christian theology. It also differs from functional divinity in its rational tendency, as well as in contrast to the experimental tendency. The Hegelian approach places the conception of God at a secondary stage within the dialectics of the absolute spirit. This means that the absolute spirit represents the reality equivalent that is obscured by the concept of God. The theory of the absolute spirit is intended to express God in the context of thought and its image.[37]

Hegel's philosophy of history is only an extension of the general theory of the absolute spirit in temporal human events, a reflection of the model and goals that the absolute spirit seeks after the organization of human consciousness into social forms (state, people, and era).[38]

2. The empiricist doctrine (neutralizing God)

English empiricism explains human knowledge and human behavior in ways that do not require theological guarantee as experi-

[35] James Collins, *God in Modern Philosophy*, 269.
[36] Peter Kossmann et al., *Atlas of Philosophy* (Oriental Library, 2011), 153.
[37] James Collins, *God in Modern Philosophy*, 370–371.
[38] Ibid., 360.

ence can dispense with God. The pioneers of this philosophical vision are Thomas Hobbes (1588–1679) and Francis Bacon (1561–1626), who emptied natural theology of all theoretical content. It is nothing but perfection mentioned in the Bible.

As for true knowledge, it is through the natural mind and senses, although the later stage of the perspective after the two pioneers was John Locke (1632–1704), who contributed to the development of a theory of knowledge in which God was not represented as a principle—even though his existence had been proven—as Locke sought to reduce God to a mere theoretical belief in his existence without any demonstrative knowledge or ethical implications,[39] the empirical method arises from a clear historical analysis of the intellectual contents of sensory perception and reflective mental processes, relying on sensory data, and the dual purpose of knowledge, controlling nature for human material welfare and fulfilling one's role competently in life.

3. Atheism (denying the existence of God)

Before the nineteenth century, the issue of denying the existence of God had not occurred to any thinker, regardless of their opinions, but this century witnessed the birth of a trend in atheism that aimed to exclude God in any way from our beliefs, openly and explicitly. Moreover, this atheistic trend or school of thought added a form of intellectual theorizing. It didn't stop at the boundaries of intellectual discussions among elite thinkers but spread to the public, leading them to adopt this atheistic thought. Also, they embraced this atheistic thought and made the methods of scientific, cultural, and moral life adapt to its implications. This atheistic thought became a point of convergence for several philosophies despite sharp disagreements on other issues.

The pioneer in this field was the materialist philosopher Ludwig Feuerbach (1804–1872), a student of Hegel and extensively familiar with his lectures on the absolute spirit. However, Feuerbach couldn't reconcile Hegel's idealistic tendency with what biology and physics were discovering about humans. Therefore, he began formulating a

[39] Ibid., 149.

philosophy that aligned with the scientific spirit of the nineteenth century, or so he claimed.

From this perspective, Feuerbach raises the issue of "alienation of God" after he criticizes Protestantism, naturalists, empiricists, and idealists. However, he sees in Hegel the precursor of this reconciliatory trend but lacks the courage to declare the inevitable conclusion that everything beyond humanity should return to humanity, and everything beyond nature should return to nature, because of Hegel's retention of the absolute spirit. After Feuerbach presents an analysis of the human mind, affirming its infinite capacity, he reaches a conclusion, stating that the mind that reaches the highest states of self-awareness should be atheistic. For Feuerbach, humans themselves are the only true God: "homo homini deus" (man is a god). Once humans understand the true meaning of religion, they can dispense with God or the absolute spirit and dedicate themselves to realizing their essential existential potential.[40]

Studies by Feuerbach intersected with atheistic tendencies. Here, we will limit ourselves within the scope of our study to briefly mention the prominent figures of this atheistic current, Marx and Nietzsche, but without forgetting to mention other prominent thinkers within this current, such as the French thinker Auguste Comte (the founder of positivist thought), the atheistic wing of existentialism (Sartre and others), logical positivism, Darwin, and others like the American naturalistic (Dewey).

Karl Marx (1818–1883) cannot be discussed in a few lines, but we will only indicate that his intellectual sources stem from the study of Epicurus, Feuerbach, and Hegel. He formulated his materialistic conception, which he termed the natural human tendency, drawing from the conviction of piety that people feel toward nature and their human contribution to civilizational achievements. He considered these reasons sufficient grounds for an atheistic stance, asserting he

---

[40] James Collins, *God in Modern Philosophy*, 378.

would not concede to any divine existence beyond nature or to any spiritual principle distinct from human intelligence and labor.[41]

Friedrich Nietzsche (1844–1900) was one of the most hostile atheists to divinity and the most influential in contemporary atheistic trends, especially the atheist wing of existential thought. He is a philosopher of power, inspiring Nazi ideology, and was influenced in his youth by the ideas of Arthur Schopenhauer (1788–1860), which encouraged his atheism.

Nietzsche's favorite image of himself is the future philosopher Hezrathustra, the wise man who descended from his mountain refuge to announce the terrible but good news of the death of God.

Nietzsche mentions that the essential message of modern atheism is not the theoretical impossibility of proving the existence of God, nor is it the actual civilizational reality that belief in God is no longer widely prevalent. The true essence of Nietzsche's anti-divine tendency lies in the fact that no one believes in God because God is no longer worthy of anyone's belief. After all, God is no longer deemed credible or worthy of human belief and support.

"What distinguishes us is not that we cannot find inspiration, whether in history, nature, or beyond nature, but rather that we now see that what we once revered as divine no longer resembles a god, but something absurd, unreasonable, harmful. It is no longer just a sin, but a crime against life. We deny God as God."[42]

American naturalism

It is necessary to point out that not all naturalistic tendencies are atheistic. The naturalistic trend emphasizes the reality of nature against cosmic tendencies, making natural existence the reference point of the universe. In this trend, there is no contradiction with God. In our modern era, the naturalistic trend opposes anything

---

[41] In our book titled *Theses on Comparative Economic Thought between the West and Islam*, published by Dar Al-Balaghah in Beirut (2015), there is an extensive discussion of dialectical materialism in Marxist thought.

[42] K. Reinhardt, "Nietzsche's Godless Existence," *Journal of Arts and Literature*, no. 3 (1951): 89–96, cited from the previous source (p. 410).

beyond or outside nature. The atheistic natural tendency, championed by Auguste Comte (1798–1857), denies the existence of divinity. It emphasizes that nothing realistic can transcend the world of sensory events and its laws. Therefore, the only absolute is our finite world. This trend was the root of the American scientific trend, as evidenced by the contemporary writings of Santayana, Dewey, Woodbridge, and Cohen. Despite the differences in their proposals, their rejection of God and personal immortality was a common theme. They asserted that nothing is above nature and that God and immortality are myths.[43]

The methodology followed by American pragmatists in knowledge is based on the empirical scientific method, and "existence is what we call nature, and nature is everything that exists."[44]

There are multiple perspectives under this title by contemporary American writers such as Rommel, Dewey, S. Hook, A. Veblen, Ayer, and so forth.

It is also worth noting the logical-empirical descriptive trend, which asserts that a statement has meaning if its truth can be verified through analysis and experiment. This method was developed in its classical form by Rudolf Carnap and Alfred Ayer. For instance, a statement like "the eternal, everlasting God, the creator of the universe" cannot be experimentally verified, thus rendering it meaningless.

Our presentation above regarding Western thought toward God was only to illustrate the intellectual background of the relationship (God, human, nature), which has produced two models. The first revolves around man as the absolute and makes him the reference point of the universe. The reference is built in the reason of humans, an ultimate human reference. The second centers around matter/nature, and humans are an integral part of nature. Therefore, the reference of nature prevails over humans with its deterministic laws, and the ultimate reference is natural and material. This result was inevitable within the context of Western thought, specifically

[43] James Collins, *God in Modern Philosophy*, 417–439.

[44] Multiple perspectives under this title by contemporary American writers such as Rommel, Dewey, S. Hook, A. Veblen, Ayer, and so forth.

liberalism, which adopted in its perspective of the universe the sum of Western intellectual theories we mentioned above.

The beginning was with the reference to humanity; which considered itself the center of solutions, dealing with it centrally around itself, without any external means of nature, declaring itself the master of the universe (i.e., its reference) and independent of nature, transcending material nature by the power of its will; and the world is perceived through the fact that man precedes nature. Western thinkers decided, according to the perspective of this model, that "human is the god of humans," as clearly presented by Max Stirner. Individuality is the center of the world, and the world, with all its things, ideas, and individuals, is only subject to this self. In other words, it appropriates the attributes of God to put them in humans.[45]

So the resulting conclusion of the first model after denying or neutralizing God, or denying his existence, came (to deify man), making him the reference point of the universe.

However, materialistic thinkers see the origin of existence as arising from a simple unformed liquid substance by sheer chance, and through a chemical reaction, it produced a single cell, which evolved according to strict laws until it became the natural material human, incapable of transcending his natural self, subject to the laws of necessity and determinism.[46]

Regardless of this view, other perspectives from Western thinkers, which view the world as a unity of existence and a single essence, some calling it "God" and others calling it "nature," present us with a completely different image of the relationship between man and nature that differs entirely from the first model.

In this view, man appears as a tiny atom amid a vast and mighty universe. Human is a material nature, and the laws of reason that distinguish humans from the rest of beings are the same as the laws of nature/material. By excluding the metaphysical and the timeless, nature and its laws become the only reference and source, even for the criteria and systems of knowledge. The human inclination is

[45] Zakaria Ibrahim, *Human Problem* (Library of Egypt), 182–183.

[46] Abdul-Wahab al-Masiri, *Partial and Comprehensive Secularism*, 242–243.

nothing but an illusion. This model, which prevailed over the first model, makes the processes of nature and its implicit laws the reference point of existence. Thus, with the removal of divinity or its neutralization, or the denial of revelation from it, Western thought this time concludes with the "deification of nature" and, consequently, the "objectification of man."

The Islamic perspective on the subject of "God, human, nature" is characterized by clarity and has not come gradually. Even though Islamic thought predates by centuries the intellectual propositions of Western thinkers, as we have discussed above, we have not witnessed any dialogue or discussion from them addressing the Islamic viewpoint. It was confined within Christian theology, indicating a lack of familiarity, if not a deliberate ignorance, of Islamic thought. This situation persists to a certain extent, despite Islamic attempts to engage with Western thought, even to this day. This underscores the ethical duty of continuous efforts to articulate the Islamic approach, which has been plagued by significant distortions through fundamentalist and terrorist movements, making it a target for Western attacks carried out through these groups and their ideologies.

The clarity of Islamic thought in the topic of our research is reinforced by three pillars:

1. Rational proof and theoretical wisdom about what we should know.
2. Faith, view, and revelation as doctrine.
3. Practical wisdom within the realities of existing reality.

Regarding the issue of existence and the Creator, in the first section, we demonstrated the rational proof of the existence of the Almighty Creator.

We find no need for repetition but to add to that the relationship between the Creator and the creature—that is, human. Existence is created, and God Almighty is necessary to exist due to the necessity of His being the creator of this existence. This existence is a real existence, but it is created. This means that Islamic thought is realistic in its view of existence, but it is created existence, and man is possible to exist through something other than Him. By the Creator, the Almighty, he is a cause, and God is the cause of his existence, and he is known by himself. "Everything known by itself is created, and everything existing in something other than itself is known. Through the creation of God Almighty, it can be inferred, and by the intellects, its knowledge is believed." This is how Imam Al-Ridha (peace be upon him) explains the issue of the Creator and the created being.[47]

And the existence of humans as an effect makes them constantly in need of their cause. However, this created being was "in the best of stature" as Allah created him distinguished by reason, making him the axis of existence. That is to say, the reference point in this universe is Allah, the Infinite Essence, and the centrality of humans with their intellect above all other creatures.

Here we mention a narration attributed to Imam Al-Sadiq (peace be upon him), where he says this: "When God created the mind, He made it articulate, then He said to it, 'Come forward,' and it came forward. Then He said to it, 'Retreat,' and it retreated. Then He said, 'By My might and majesty, I have not created a creation that is more beloved to Me than you, nor have I completed anyone except in the one I love. Indeed, I command you, and I prohibit you, and I punish you, and I reward you.'"[48]

The second aspect comes through the perspective of humans, which Allah has naturally inclined them toward, through their faith in Allah and religion.

"So, direct your face toward the religion, inclining to truth. [Adhere to] the fitrah of Allah upon which He has created [all] people. No change should there be in the creation of Allah. That is the correct religion, but most of the people do not know."[49]

This nature was strengthened by God (through divine enlightenment) to know the universe and existence through revelation and the messengers and prophets: "Indeed, we have sent among you a

---

[47] Mohammad Taqi al-Modarresi, *Islamic Mysticism* (Balagh Foundation, 1988), 298.

[48] Muhammad ibn Yaaqub al-Kulayni, *Principles of Al-Kafi* (Al-Adwa Publishing House, 1992), 1:57–58.

[49] Surah Al-Roum, verse 30.

Messenger from yourselves reciting to you Our verses and purifying you and teaching you the Book and wisdom and teaching you that which you did not know."[50]

"And He is the Most Merciful. He taught the Quran, created man, and taught him eloquence."[51]

The third dimension is determined by practical wisdom through a human's relationship with nature. Humans, in any era, have not surrendered to nature and have been subject to it and its forces. Rather, he is trying, at every time and place, to impose himself on nature, limit the power of its forces, and assert his right to exist as an axis around which other worlds revolve. It is part of nature as a body (matter and form) that comprehends the world as a mind and spirit. Experience teaches us that humans can modify, refine, and adjust their environment to meet their evolving and changing needs. Scientific knowledge and industrial technical developments are merely mere means. Humans use it to enhance their abilities to control the natural environment in which they live. The important thing is not that he adapts to the world but rather that the world adapts to him, thanks to his mental ability that does not accept natural data as it is. Hence, the attribute of transcendence and centrality is attributed to humans. The universe alone is unable to balance its calculations and is always waiting for a man to give him balance and meaning.[52]

Through this presentation, we see the Islamic perspective, which views Allah as the Creator and the ultimate reference point of this universe. It also recognizes humans as distinguished creatures endowed with intellect, created in the best of stature, and illuminated by divine guidance through revelation. This makes humans the focal point of this world, capable of adapting nature and striving to control it, ultimately seeking worldly happiness.

---

[50] Surah Al-Baquarah, verse 151.

[51] Surah Al-Rahman, verses 1–4.

[52] G. Gusdorf, *Traité de Métaphysiques* (Paris-Colin, 1955), 62–63. From Zakaria Ibrahim, *Human Problem*, 58.

Chapter 3

Freedom of Will

A human's relationship with himself, with others, with society, with nature, and with God are dimensions addressed by the concepts of freedom and the perspective from which thought begins to determine the will, and thus to create action. Freedom is the basic pillar of the will, meaning that it is the causality that makes the will able to act without external coercion, which is described as a negative interpretation of freedom as presented by some philosophers. In contrast, the thinker Immanuel Kant refers to the positive meaning of freedom, as the perception of causality involves the perception of laws that require necessity. To accept, through something we call a cause, something else we call a result, so freedom, although it is not, in fact, a property that characterizes the will according to the laws of nature, cannot for this reason be devoid of all laws. Rather, it is better to say that it must be an entity that proceeds in its actions according to laws that do not change, even if these laws are of a special type. Otherwise, freedom would be an impossible thing.[53]

The issue of freedom is a fundamental pillar whose branches extend to the issues of science, ethics, society, economics, and politics in addition to its absolute, contemplative, metaphysical concept. In this study, we will not go into examining concrete descriptive free-

[53] Immanuel Kant, *Foundations of Metaphysics of Morals* (National Printing and Publishing House, 1965), 103.

doms and their realistic problems that relate to specific freedoms and in specific times and places. Instead, we will focus in the subsequent sections of this work, on exploring freedom within the framework of economics, dedicating the necessary space to it as an example of situational freedoms, aligning with the theme of our study in economic thought. As for the concept of freedom in its absolute, contemplative, and metaphysical sense, it is the approach that we will address in these introductions to the philosophical background of Islamic thought as a contemplative framework for theoretical reason and as a determinant of the approach to practical reason to avoid deviations.

Materialistic and situational thought, including individualistic liberal thought and the new liberalism, tend to prioritize freedom of capability over freedom of will in their conceptual frameworks and intellectual orientations. This inclination is a natural outcome of their intellectual background, which relies on empirical sources of knowledge, as discussed in the previous section. Conversely, rationalistic thought, in its analyses, tends to focus on freedom of will, which is also a natural consequence of its reliance on metaphysical and intellectual sources of knowledge.

This does not mean that liberal thought limits its perspectives according to specific universal criteria; rather, within the same intellectual framework, there are variations in approaches, analyses, and objectives, including liberal thought and even Islamic thought. Therefore, in the context of this work, it is necessary to address some liberal thinkers according to the research requirements when discussing topics related to freedom of will.

As for Islamic thought, our central topic, we are not going to present the intellectual differences among its intellectual schools of thought, but rather, we will start from the fact that freedom is an important indicator of the development of Islamic thought and its ability to renew in our contemporary reality, and therefore, what we will go to is nothing but an extrapolation of the thought and spirit of Islam and its contemporary data based on the origins of Islamic thought.

Researching the topic of freedom deeply and objectively necessitates addressing the intellectual framework that makes "freedom" a concept, particularly liberalism, which the thinker Abdullah al-Arwi claims, "Liberalism considers freedom the principle and the goal, the motive and the result, the origin, and the outcome in human life. It is the only intellectual system that aspires for nothing but describing human activity freely, explaining its aspects and commenting on it."[54]

It is crucial to understand the concept of freedom in liberal thought to address its perspective on human beings and their evolution or, rather, their changes, and where it stands in contemporary reality. This examination sheds light on its practical implications and performance contexts, prompting us to present it below.

In the stages of the formation of liberal thought, two models address humans and nature within the framework of inherent reference, starting with humanity and culminating in nature. The first model revolves around the human, believing in it as absolute and central to the universe, with the ultimate reference for humans. These contexts end with the other model centered on matter and nature, where the human is a part of this nature, and the reference is inherent in material nature.

Modern liberal philosophy, described as humanistic liberalism, fully emphasizes humanity and its centrality above nature, considering it as its ultimate reference. This philosophy revolves around the self, which is boundless, capable of generating cognitive systems and transcending religion and moral systems without the need for any divine revelation—the divinity of which we will address in later parts of this work. Consequently, it is characterized by

- centering around the self and the illusion of its triumph over the subject;
- viewing the universe as latent within humanity;
- considering humanity as the measure of all things, with will as the will of power;
- excessive individualism and rejection of all abstractions and universalities.[55]

---

[54] Abdullah al-Arwi, *The Concept of Freedom* (Arab Cultural Center, 2012), 49.

[55] Abdul-Wahab al-Masiri, *Partial and Comprehensive Secularism* (Al-Shorouq Publishing House, 2002), 263–270.

The individualistic focus on the self inevitably leads to individualism, which has been a significant feature of liberal thought. Self-interest, personal benefit, and confrontation with others formed the cumulative beginnings for the emergence of imperialistic humanism.

On the other hand, the liberal approach of deconstruction and composition, which stems from a materialistic and non-humanistic perspective, is nature-matter, excluding everything spiritual and beyond measurement and sensory perception, transcending materialism. It sees in humans only what is material, with a single dimension, part of nature subject to its laws and determinism. Consequently, humans become a set of natural desires and motives governed by the same laws that apply to things, with nature as their ultimate reference. This intellectual background deals with the birth of the world as coincidental, its chemical and organic interaction, and humans are merely products of this process, descendants of apes as Darwin suggested. Therefore, the inevitable outcome of this perspective is the centrality of material nature and its latent reference, with humans being an integral part of nature—living according to its laws, thus becoming something subject to the logic of nature.

Therefore, we notice the shift in the direction of this thought, which in its beginnings placed humans in the center of (God), only to return to make him (a thing) in front of (the deification of nature). In presenting this thought with integrity and honesty, it is essential to mention the significant writings of liberal thinkers who solidified the intellectual approach and placed it within the practical contexts of neoliberalism's direct interaction with the world. This was expressed by the American contemporary thinker Rorty as a project to remove divinity or holiness from the world and for humans to accept the temporality of everything.[56]

The absolute material, natural human who lives according to these absolute natural laws derives knowledge, values, and even aesthetics solely from them. This is what Hobbes referred to with his strict materialism, the wolflike ethics of humans, Locke on the

---

[56] Ibid., 277.

human mind, Bentham in the doctrine of utility and pleasure,[57] Spinoza's monistic materialism, and so forth.[58]

Here, it remains important to highlight the key characteristics of this natural, materialistic approach, as we mentioned above for the characteristics of the self-centered approach:

- Gradual dissolution of the self into nature and its disappearance, leading to the triumph of the object.
- The center of the universe lies within nature, which becomes the reference point for everything, including humans, resulting in the loss of human centrality.
- Material laws govern humans just as they govern nature, thus asserting the dominance of materialistic natural determinism.
- Humans are part of nature, and therefore they harness themselves in service to the object.
- Emphasis on the external world and consequently the flattening of things.[59]

What we have presented regarding the liberal thought trajectory provides the intellectual perspective on the concept of freedom among liberals, from the era of modernization to contemporary new liberalism, as proposed by Hayek, who confines it to the freedom of capability, emphasizing the ability of the will to generate action in social, economic, and political aspects (such as participating in government selection, satisfying individual desires, etc.).[60]

After this necessary deviation to present some aspects of liberal thought, we return to our main course of presenting, analyzing, and discussing the metaphysical concept of freedom.

---

[57] Ibid., 238.
For further information, see the previous source (volume 1).

[58] For further information, see the previous source, (volume 1). Previous source, 264–265.

[59] Abdul-Wahab al-Masiri, *Partial and Comprehensive Secularism*, 264–265.

[60] Anthony de Crespigny and Kenneth Minogue, *Figures of Contemporary Political Philosophy* (Egyptian Book Authority, 1996), 41–57.

To discuss the issue of freedom in a scientific methodology, we start from the possibility of creating action and the extent of freedom that the cause of creating action has in the ability to create it—that is, the will, which is the cause of action. What is its extent of freedom in its ability to create the possibility of existence for action? It is met with an opposition that prevents the will from being characterized by freedom when it is possible to create action. This opposition carries the meanings of necessity, determinism, or compulsion and thus denies freedom of action. Therefore, if freedom of the will is not met with an opposition that prevents its existence, its discussion becomes meaningless.

Therefore, it is necessary for the beginning to understand the meaning of necessity and inevitability and the extent of their reflection on freedom of will.

In the philosophical sense, necessity is what must be, meaning it is inevitable or obligatory. In a general sense, it becomes a universal law according to which life must proceed within its contexts.

Thus, those who seek primacy and centrality of nature lean toward determinism or concepts of fate and predestination or even coercion, where the comprehensive natural laws fulfill their will regardless of human will. Here, we refer to the writings of Western thinkers in the modern era, such as Hobbes, Hume, Stuart Mill, and Herbert Spencer (from the seventeenth century to the twentieth century). Hobbes refers to natural freedom and the capacity for will, suggesting they are mere illusions without foundation. Meanwhile, Hume explicitly asserts the dominance of necessity in human actions, thereby denying free will.

The philosopher of freedom in the French Revolution, Voltaire, does not depart from this trending subject to the will of nature despite his vehement defense of freedom in practical application, despite denying freedom in the theoretical realm from a metaphysical perspective: "We are wheels in a great machine, and our minds think as if they were free because this feeling of freedom is itself a wheel in that machine." Thus Voltaire views will.[61]

[61] Zakaria Ibrahim, *Philosophical Problems / Problem of Freedom* (Library of Egypt, 1963), 57.

These references to Western writings don't necessarily imply the absence of other currents in interpreting free will, even within the liberal doctrine itself.

Indeed, some rationalists believe that the best things are necessarily by reason. It's very useful to mention here the philosopher Immanuel Kant, who considers free will, in its autonomous independence, as one of the principles of ethical laws.

"What could freedom of will be, if it is not self-independence, that is, the property that distinguishes will and makes it a law unto itself... Thus, free will and will subject to ethical laws are the same thing."[62]

Alongside natural determinism, there emerge intellectual dimensions that address what is called theological determinism, which speaks of human submission to the divine will in an absolute manner, thus rendering this determinism "compulsory," affirming predestination and fate. While some Western thinkers within a religious framework have espoused this perspective, certain Islamic sects have also carved out this trajectory. It suffices here to mention the Jahmiyyah, a theological school that justified the Umayyad authority's dominance. They expressed their view as follows:

> Human is not capable of everything, nor is he described by capability, but he is compelled in his actions without his power or choice. Rather, Allah creates actions in him according to what He creates in all inanimate objects. Actions are attributed to Him metaphorically, as they are attributed to inanimate objects. It is said: the tree bore fruit, the water flowed, the stone moved, the sun rose and set, the sky clouded and rained, the earth bloomed and sprouted, and so on.[63]

---

[62] Immanuel Kant, *Foundations of Metaphysics of Morals* (National Printing and Publishing House, 1965), 104.

[63] Ahmed Amin, *Doha al-Islam*, 2nd ed. (1941), 44–61. From Zakaria Ibrahim, *Philosophical Problems / Problem of Freedom*, 152–153.

The intellectual foundation of this trajectory is based on the premise that if humans are creators of their actions, does this imply the existence of another creator alongside Allah?

And there cannot be a partner to Allah. This is what the Western thinker Malebranche expressed in a contrasting manner: "Man, by himself, is pure nothingness...he cannot think or move without Allah... Therefore, Allah is the creator of our thoughts, our essence, and our pains."[64]

Christian thinkers have attempted to reconcile human will in the freedom of choice with the will of God, suggesting that humans are only truly free when their will aligns with the freedom of will of God. This is expressed in what is called "the theory of natural predestination" by Thomas Aquinas, which essentially states that God wills all our actions in a certain way but also wills them to be free at the same time. In other words, if I perform a certain action with my absolute freedom, it is as God wills it to be. Thus, we can say that these human actions have been eternally predestined by God to be free as if they are both predetermined and free at the same time?

In addition to our previous reference to the French Cartesian thinker Malebranche, it is necessary to mention here the liberal thinker Spinoza, who unifies natural necessity and divine will. The divine will imposes a necessity on nature, making it impossible for anything to occur or happen outside this divine necessity. Thus, everything in nature is subject to the necessity of divine nature.

The reason is the source of forming the will, meaning that the will is a mental process based on understanding motives and the nature of influences. Therefore, freedom should characterize the will to negate any external compulsion from the true principle of action creation. In other words, action is what connects thought and existence through the will. In this sense, the will is the tool of connection between the self and the object. It presupposes freedom because it is nothing but the realization of human agency about nature, which creates a gap between desire and its fulfillment. Thus, the will, elevated by thought

---

[64] C. F. Malebranche, *Meditations Chretiènnes*. From Zakaria Ibrahim, *Philosophical Problems / Problem of Freedom*, 152–153.

and defined by freedom, requires achievable effort, overcoming resistance, and reaching a specific goal as determined by thought.

Descartes made "thought" the primary technical truth upon which all other truths are based as it is merely a possibility dependent on the freedom of will to generate the existence of action, which in turn is subject to capability. The direct correlation between the self and external existence is realized through action, which strips the self of its meaning, reveals its value, and confirms its existence. Thus, in action, we see an expression of the unity of thought and will and an indication of the close connection between self and existence.[65]

With utmost precision, it is essential to distinguish between the actual perspective of philosophical doctrines regarding the inevitability of nature, destiny, and determinism and the materialistic and situational doctrines, including liberalism and theology (as presented above). Philosophical doctrines do not necessarily imply that true freedom and freedom of will are entirely independent of natural necessity. Instead, they are based on reason and contemplative knowledge, along with their relationship to practical knowledge, to understand the laws to exploit them to achieve specific goals through systematic methods based on intellectual development. They emphasize the importance of things that align with reason and are necessarily realized.

Freedom presupposes the presence of reason, which distinguishes between causes and goals, making free action the result of rational reasons. Without these reasons, there would be no need to talk about freedom. As thought evolves with knowledge and scientific advancements, its ability to understand and utilize necessities increases. It can even harness them for its purposes as defined by its goals.

Hence, Descartes argued: "Our will inclines neither towards seeking nor fleeing anything except as our minds portray it to us, either favorably or unfavorably. Therefore, it is sufficient for a person to judge well to act well, and to judge in the best way possible to act promptly and effectively."[66]

---

65 Zakaria Ibrahim, *Philosophical Problems / Problem of Freedom*, 179.

66 Zakaria Ibrahim, *Philosophical Problems / Problem of Freedom*, 185.

Thought expresses an infinite capacity of the self to envision possibilities beyond what nature presents to us. Nature, in turn, is rationalized by thought, unable to reduce the human self to a mere cog in its cosmic machinery. Contemplation alone can empower the human self with a newfound ability to surpass all natural limitations and boundaries. Hence, the philosopher Immanuel Kant was correct in asserting that the self always feels its loftiness and superiority over every natural principle within it, including its instincts, desires, and habits. However, the task of the self is not limited to overcoming the natural principle but rather to exploiting it and working to benefit from it.[67]

This is the path that dethrones necessity from the throne of nature, transforming it from a commanding mistress into an obedient servant to that rational, thoughtful, and free self.

So freedom in the intellectual sense, meaning the supremacy of reason over will, can only exist where this intellectual capacity and the intentional action have real meaning, enabling humans to achieve things that nature alone would not permit. Human thought and humanity will be the sole means for the emergence of new things in the world. Conversely, if freedom of will were to disappear in favor of nature, the human self would descend to the level of mechanization while nature's supremacy would reach its peak. Our responses would then become mere products of external influences.

This evolving intellectual tendency toward metaphysical freedom is affirmed by scientific advancement and knowledge in our current century, leading human thought back to the concept of human development. This stands in contrast to neoliberal thought, which tends to view knowledge as a reflection of materialism or submission to natural determinism, thus avoiding acknowledgment of a metaphysical theory of freedom. Instead, it focuses on issues of power in matters related to social, economic, and political freedom, among others.

It's not surprising that contemporary neoliberal thinkers like Hayek focus more on practical and descriptive concepts rather than theory, as we discussed earlier in their interpretation of the meaning of freedom.

---

67 Ibid., 191.

Freedom in Islamic thought

Our main topic within the scope of researching freedom, particularly from the perspective of Islam as a rational doctrine, the concept of freedom takes on an absolute metaphysical meaning. Therefore, the axis of reason, will, and potentiality or capability are fundamental issues addressed according to its intellectual perspective. It's also essential to determine the Islamic stance on issues that appear to contradict freedom, such as necessity and predestination. Furthermore, a crucial and fundamental issue that must be addressed is the precise relationship between thought and the requirements of Sharia law and how this reflects on the system of freedom.

The following issues will be addressed in our work in this field. We have decided to include an important topic related to practical wisdom, even though our work primarily focuses on the intellectual and metaphysical aspects of freedom. This exception is made due to the significance of the topic, which is the issue of "slavery."

The deduction method we follow to determine the judgment or stance of Islamic thought on the issues we present is based on the themes of revelation through the Quran, the traditions of the Prophet (PBUH), and the household of the Prophet (PBUH) and reliable sources from the chosen companions and the ijtihad of established scholars in both knowledge and prominent thinkers. It's not necessarily to infer from contexts of existing Islamic systems because we are seeking what should be, not what is existing. Moreover, the context of research in Islamic thought according to the deduction method should fundamentally rely on the spiritual perspective of thought, avoiding a partial or selective perspective of specific facts. In other words, references will only be within the contexts of the spiritual formative trend of Islam with its holistic meanings, dimensions, and objectives and an elevated vision of theoretical wisdom.

A methodical reading of the literature of Islamic thought, as we have referred to above, within the contexts of its spiritual deduction, does not require much effort to conclude that Islamic thought, in its essence, affirms that humans are inherently endowed with freedom—meaning that freedom is a component of human nature, inherent and not incidental. Its manifestations are found in intellectual and rational issues, as well as in the freedom of thought.

"So, whoever wills, let him believe; and whoever wills, let him disbelieve."[68]

Its most prominent manifestation is in the famous saying of Imam Ali ibn Abi Talib (PBUH): "O my Lord, I did not worship You out of fear of Your Fire, nor out of desire for Your Paradise; rather, I saw You worthy of worship, so I worshipped You."

The pinnacle of victorious freedom of thought and mental conviction is embodied by Imam Ali in this saying: "I have not found anything more profound in the literature I have encountered regarding the freedom of thought. It is a freedom of thought in its purest form, as clear as daylight."

"Have you not given your interpretation of it, or have the people made it possible for you to interpret it as if they were not believers?"[69]

In parallel with thought, divine law (Sharia) serves as a guide for some, raising questions as a delineator of thought. This necessitates illumination within the context of this research. We can say that the knowledge of the divine cosmic order, as we have previously discussed, has provided ample space for reason alongside divine law. As we stated earlier, there is no contradiction between reason and divine law. From this perspective, divine law serves as divine enlightenment for the intellect, preventing it from stumbling and erring and guiding human behavior and methodology. Its approach has never been one of coercion or compulsion but rather one of advice, persuasion, choice, and warning, aiming for the elevation of human behavior to the level for which it was created to the highest standard. In this context, the issue of predestination (Qadar) was not an obligatory matter of fate.

Nothing is more illustrative of this than the narration attributed to Imam Ali (PBUH) to ibn Nabata and his statement:

> Perhaps you thought of it as a compelling decree and an inevitable destiny. If it were

[68] Surah Al-Kahf, verse 29.

[69] Surah Younis, verse 99.

> so, then the system of reward and punishment, promise and warning, and prohibition would be nullified. No one would be rewarded for good deeds, and no one would be held accountable for sins. The doer of good would not deserve praise, nor would the sinner deserve blame. Indeed, Allah the Almighty has commanded choice and prohibited wrong, and He has made the burden light, not insurmountable. He did not command obedience from the vanquished, nor did He compel the unwilling. He did not send messengers in vain...[70]

According to this context, the intellect becomes a beneficiary of divine law and wisdom. In other words, divine enlightenment, or Sharia, becomes a guide for paths, life methodologies, and human behavior. The intellect accepts it with full conviction and freedom, rejecting any compulsion or determinism. Thus, for the believer in the message of Islam, freedom of thought is integrated with both reason and divine law.

Thought is the premise for willpower. Willpower is consensus and determination, a voluntary inclination. It may exist by choice or by compulsion, but necessity here is adaptable and consistent with reason. Therefore, in conceptualizing the intellect and defining the concept of the premise, it operates according to specific laws in the divine cosmic system that must be understood. Otherwise, freedom of will becomes meaningless. Acquiring knowledge that determines willpower can only be achieved through free thought as we have defined it.

Willpower is the affirmative mode of the reason. No external action or movement is initiated by a person intentionally unless its principle arises from within oneself, passing through all its interme-

---

70 Nasir al-Din Muhammad ibn Hasan al-Tusi, *The Disclosure of the Intended in Abstracting Belief*, 2:294.

diate levels and faculties between the soul and the manifestation of its actions and the mechanism of its motion.[71]

It is assumed that when a person intends to perform an action or movement, they must first know by envisioning that action and believing in its benefit. Then they must have the will and determination for it, followed by a desire and eagerness. Finally, there must be an inclination in their faculties toward achieving it.[72]

Free will to act must entail capability or ability. The meaning of the capability is that whenever we wish and there is no obstacle, we act.[73]

However, the chosen action is what moves from potentiality to actuality. It requires a determining factor that moves the choice from potentiality to actuality, either an internal inclination prompting it or an external factor. In this case, the chosen action is under the judgment of necessity, but in the manner we indicated by the harmony of necessity with reason.

Here it is necessary to address the discussion that has arisen regarding the issue of free will, capability to act, and their relationship to divine authority. Some Islamic sects have interpreted free will and the ability to act as a negation of divine authority!

In this context, we present the following. There is no dispute regarding the meaning of free will as we have indicated earlier and in understanding the necessity of its existence. In the context of capability, possibility, and therefore existence and continuity and the ability to act, we say this. The existence of Allah, glorified and exalted, is necessary for Himself and Himself, while the existence of others is necessary through Him, not in themselves.[74]

Therefore, the existence of human beings and the necessity of their existence are through Allah, and the need for the effect of the cause is continuity. Thus, the will is free, and the possibility of action based on capability is the causative force that always requires its cause.

---

[71] Sadr al-Din al-Shirazi, *Supreme Wisdom in the Four Journeys*, 2:609.

[72] Ibid., 610.

[73] Ibid., 592.

[74] Ibid., 605.

Consequently, we affirm the absence of any contradiction between free will and the authority of the Creator, as suggested by some.

In the context of divine wisdom and guidance, divine enlightenment, and guiding human behavior, actions were categorized into obligatory, recommended, permissible, disliked, and prohibited. The permissible refers to actions where neither praise nor blame is attached to doing or refraining from them. The obligatory refers to actions deserving of praise when done and blame when neglected. The recommended refers to actions deserving of praise when done but without blame attached to neglecting them. The disliked refers to actions deserving of praise when refrained from but without blame attached to doing them. Additionally, there are prohibited actions, which require abstention from them.[75]

Here, the exceptional indication we mentioned in the context of practical reason comes into play. From the Islamic perspective, according to the context we presented, why wouldn't it be preferable to classify "slavery" as one of the prohibited actions, meaning the absence of any explicit text prohibiting slavery as a form of human servitude to another human?

In this context, and as an opinion not based on any jurisprudential reference, it is an interpretation that relies on reasoning through observing the social environment surrounding the location where the revelation descended and, consequently, the Islamic message. The divine wisdom in addressing the resulting phenomena within the context of human life. The society of the Arabian Peninsula, with its economic activities primarily based on pastoralism and certain crafts, heavily relied on slavery. A direct prohibition of slavery would have dramatically destabilized the societal structure with unpredictable consequences. Therefore, Islam indirectly addressed this issue by encouraging the manumission of slaves, even making it a means of expiation for sins. Through a prudent and wise approach within a specific historical context, Islam was able to gradually eliminate this practice without causing dramatic upheavals in society.

---

[75] Nasir al-Din Muhammad ibn Hasan al-Tusi, *The Disclosure of the Intended in Abstracting Belief*, 280.

Chapter 4

The Concept of the State

Some contemporary thinkers argue that the state is a reality in our era. It controls various aspects of our lives, issues laws, and imposes taxes. Nevertheless, people do not question or doubt the authority of the state in doing these things; it is almost considered granted as one of the principles of existence. Therefore, these thinkers see no benefit in exploring the theory of the state and its origins. Rather, the focus should be on the form of the state, its performance, and the legitimacy of its practices.

This opinion confines scientific research to one aspect under the pretext of dealing realistically with the basic realities of existence. In our scientific perspective, we move beyond merely studying the phenomenon. Comprehensive and intellectual comprehension compels us to delve into the ontology, emergence, and purpose thereof, along with the various approaches to formation and the legitimacy of the approach. Therefore, it is essential to address the theory of the state not in the specific sense of a particular state but in the absolute sense, considering the factors of emergence and the goals it seeks to achieve. It allows us to pass judgments within its theoretical framework, paving the way for practical wisdom in what should be done. Moreover, it helps to define the purpose in alignment with reason, determine the legitimacy of the approach and how to correct and evaluate deviations. Thus, these determinants must be addressed in our research, especially considering the added impetus of researching in economic fields, where the state plays a fundamental role. This topic gains crucial significance in our current era regarding what is happening in our contemporary world and the role the state should play in people's economic lives.

Humans are social creatures; they cannot live and continue life individually. This condition may be innate. Humans may not uniquely possess this trait but, in a narrower sense, structurally, methodologically, and in pattern. Some animals also exhibit this communal characteristic, as seen in the animal kingdom of bees and ants. However, this is driven by specific animal instincts that remain primitive and unevolved. In contrast, for humans, instinct serves as a foundation upon which the pillars of development and the impetus for advancement are built, aiming for the best forms conducive to their adaptation and happiness in life.

However, is this premise of the theory of Humans as social beings sufficient to make him a basis for the endeavor to establish the state, where it is believed that his affairs and life approach can only be upright in the presence of the state? Certainly, the matter is not confined to this aspect alone. Human beings have dimensions with others and society, and since their dimensions are not limited solely to material life, there are spiritual and intellectual dimensions seeking the essence of existence and striving for the best forms of individual, societal, and existential relationships, both created and thus the Creator.

In general, theoretical currents among thinkers have tried to define the concept of "the state." Is it a natural entity like human institutions such as the family and tribe, or is it an artificial construct invented by the human mind under the pressure of material life requirements and through experience? Or is there another perspective that justifies the existence of the state? For objectivity in the context of our scientific research, we should not confine the determination to Islamic thought alone. Rather, we should consider the intellectual perspectives of prominent global thought currents. Just as we previously focused on Western thinkers as they constitute the intellectual background of liberal thought, which is prevalent in most countries today. It does not mean ignoring viewpoints from intellectual currents that have played a significant role in shaping lifestyles. Rather, we narrow our focus to the purpose of scientific research aimed at presenting Islamic thought in comparison to dominant liberalism, which shapes the reality and potential of many countries in facing the challenges of existence, life, and even nature.

The approach of Western thinkers to the concept of the state is coherent, even an extension of their perspective on the concept of "humanity," which we discussed in section 2 of this study. Moreover, the universal features of Western liberal thought fall within the concepts of individualism and utilitarianism—subjects we will address later in the presentation and critique. Therefore, the context of the concept of the state is determined accordingly. We will review the most prominent Western thinkers on this subject, noting the variation in their approaches but the convergence in the essence of the idea.

According to Hobbes, the state is not natural. It is artificial, a product of individuals' actions. He sees humans as wolves to one another, where their natural existence is marked by ferocity, fear, envy, and plotting harm against others. Their lives revolve around the pursuit of their desires. Therefore, morality, for Hobbes, is relative to the satisfaction of human desires and utility. Satisfying desires is necessary for life's continuation, and thus, rationality and deliberation are necessary in their conflicts with others, which inevitably lead to cooperation for the satisfaction of individual desires. This compels humans to enter a social contract where they relinquish some of their freedoms in exchange for a power that ensures their security and the realization of their desires, as Hobbes terms it, the "social contract."

Bentham leans toward this direction as well, but his premise is that humans are naturally inclined to choose and are not wolves as Hobbes decrees. However, Hegel's concept of the state takes a different trajectory. The state is not only about preserving individuals' interests; its goal is to achieve perfection, both absolute and spiritual. According to Hegel, the individual preserves his freedom, his existential reality, and his humanity only by being a member of the state. Through Hegel's writings, particularly in *Philosophy of Law*, the state is an expression of absolute spirit, an actualized free will in and for itself, not contingent upon anything external. Hegel even goes as far as to consider the state as God's representative on earth (the deification of the state),[76] where the state is the objective idea, the moral spirit that manifests itself knows itself and accomplishes what it knows because it knows it.[77] It's a deductive result, an abstraction of facts. This is Hegel's perspective, which contrasts with thinkers of the "social contract" theory, whom he rejects.

The prominent theorization of the concept of the state comes from Jean-Jacques Rousseau, through his theory of the social contract. This theory assumes implicitly that individuals voluntarily, for their interests and benefit, establish a contract among themselves wherein they relinquish a portion of their freedom in exchange for the establishment of a higher general administration that ensures them a secure life and the fulfillment of their desires. "Each of us puts his person and all his power in common under the supreme direction of the general will, and we also accept each member as an indivisible part of the whole."[78] Thus, what the individual loses through the social contract is his natural freedom and the unlimited right he had to everything he desired, gained, and could access, while what he gains is civil liberty and ownership of all that he possesses.[79] Therefore, according to this social contract (which is not an event that happened but an implicit assumption), the authority or right to command is bestowed upon the body emanating from it, and the individual's role is merely obedience and submission. Here, Rousseau assumes that this authority or power granted to the body must be coupled with rights so that individual obedience becomes a duty.

Theories of the state are supposed to provide insights into the reality of the state's emergence. Isn't this the scientific approach even demanded by empiricists, positivists, and materialists? In the actual emergence of the state, we find another direction, especially with the theory of the social contract, which contemporary thinker Robert

---

[76] Ahmad Zaher, *Studies in Political Philosophy*, 54–56.

[77] Abdullah al-Arwi, *The Concept of the State* (Arab Cultural Center, 1993), 25.

[78] Jean-Jacques Rousseau, *The Social Contract* (Oriental Library, 2016), 29.

[79] Ibid., 34.

Carneiro considers a historical anecdote.[80] Carneiro provides two scientific foundations for the emergence of the state according to the theories that have addressed the emergence of states.

The first perspective is based on the freedom of will and agreement (including the theory of the social contract), while the other perspective sees the emergence of the state based on violence and coercion and excludes the theory of the social contract due to the lack of a realistic basis, as no contract was ever made or signed. Attention turns to the modern voluntarist theory, through what is known as "mechanical voluntarist theory." This theory discusses the socioeconomic development of society through the evolution of agriculture, the accumulation of surplus, the emergence of craftsmanship, and social progression, which automatically led to the establishment of the state. Key contemporary writings on this subject include those by the British author Gordon Childe and Karl Witt Fogel.

Carneiro concluded that voluntarist theories are inadequate in addressing the issue of violence in the historical explanation of the emergence of the state.

As for the perspective attributing the emergence of the state to violence and coercion, it provides evidence of wars that played various forms of a fundamental role in the emergence of the state across the globe.[81] One of the prominent contemporary theorists of this perspective is Edward Genghis.

Another perspective on the emergence of the state through historical observation of the lives of peoples and societies combines the essential volitional aspects necessary for the development of societies alongside conflicts and warfare, as presented by the contemporary thinker Julius Lips.[82] In a preceding overview of the lives of different peoples from various parts of the world, Lips illustrates how life was organized within the tribe, not concerning other population centers but rather the internal organization of tribal life, the generation of

---

[80] R. L. Carneiro, *A Theory on the Emergence of the State* (Akademie-Verlag, 1973), 153–174.

[81] R. L. Carneiro, *A Theory on the Emergence of the State*, 10.

[82] Julius Lips, *The Origin of Things* (Al-Madinah for Culture and Publishing, 2006), 259–286.

laws regulating it, and the provision of means of livelihood. He then moves on to the external relations with population centers, discussing conflicts, agreements, and the organization resembling modern-day external relations. All these are patterns conducive to the emergence of the state.

Here, we cannot overlook the view presented by the contemporary existentialist thinker Bertrand Russell in his book *Power and the Individual*, attributing the emergence of the state to the community's need for cohesion, achieved through a sense of an external enemy. This cohesion necessitated the establishment of a mechanism to reach social decisions, which inevitably evolved over stages into what modern humans recognize as government.[83]

The Islamic perspective on the concept and emergence of the state relies on three dimensions:

1) The theory of existence and creation, as discussed in section 1 of this study, and divine guidance and revelation.
2) The creative human reason is in its continuous evolutionary state.
3) Practical realities derived from experience.

In the field of existence, the divine cosmic system does not merely address the individual conscience briefly, nor are its dimensions confined to the spiritual realm alone. Rather, it integrates the worldly life of the individual with the spiritual dimension extending to the afterlife. In the worldly dimension, the capability to confront the demands of earthly life is manifested by divine enlightenment. The innate social nature of humans serves as a starting point for the process of development, determining the pattern of the relationship between the individual and the community. Within this transitional scope, the state emerges as an inevitable necessity for the advancement and progress of society within the divine cosmic system.

---

[83] Bertrand Russell, *Authority and the Individual* (Al-Taliah Publishing House, 1961), 40.

In the field of existence, the divine cosmic order was not a brief address to the individual conscience, nor were its dimensions limited to the spiritual dimension.

Rather, the individual's worldly life is integrated with the spiritual dimension extending to the afterlife. The worldly dimension manifests itself in the ability to face the requirements of worldly life by divine enlightenment. Human social nature is the starting point for a process of development that determines the pattern of the relationship between the individual and the group, and within the interim scope, the state comes as an inevitable necessity for the development and advancement of society within the divine cosmic order.

As for the human reason, Islam does not extend the scope of revelation and religious law to cover all practical domains within the realm of worldly development. Instead, it leaves their determination and interpretation to human reason and experience (practical wisdom), guided by theoretical wisdom, where there is interaction between reason, knowledge, wisdom, and Sharia. This interaction aims to delineate the domains for each mode of life in a balanced manner, making the perspective comprehensive for refining human behavior and developing life. The position of reason in Islamic thought and the clarity of its functional contexts have been pivotal in understanding the emergence of civilization over transient periods.

In the third dimension, Islam's belief in the law of evolution and renewal knows no bounds. Here, we point to its calls for renewal not only in worldly matters but also in religious affairs. While the religious reference pertains to revelation and divine teachings, Islam is not solely a spiritual religion. Instead, it offers a comprehensive perspective where religious principles interact with divine enlightenment and the imperatives of intellectual and scientific development. This interaction shapes a creative pattern in harmony with the authority of reason and human experience, governed by the interests of both individuals and the community.

Although the state is a requirement according to the divine cosmic system, it represents a rational context for the developmental pattern of society. The best things in necessity align with the dictates of reason. From this, we can deduce that in Islamic thought, the state is a requirement according to the divine cosmic system. It intersects with the innovations of reason as a developmental pattern for society, serving as a practical response to the interests of both individuals and the community in developing their way of life and achieving happiness connected to their aspirations for the afterlife.

Here, we must mention the circumstances under which the Islamic state emerged, not for the sake of historical analysis but to provide insights that align with the perspective we have presented. By the end of the sixth century CE, the Byzantine Empire, adhering to Christianity, and the Persian Empire, adhering to Zoroastrianism, dominated most of the Middle East. In their shadow, the message of Islam is conveyed by the noble Prophet (PBUH).

The Arabs, scattered across the Arabian Peninsula, embroiled in tribal conflicts and harsh desert conditions, held no significance or influence in the political and social landscape under the dominance of these empires. In such an environment, the message of Islam, delivered by an unlettered prophet, unified them in faith, increasing their faith and determination. In a remarkably short time, the Islamic state emerged, spreading across three continents. In such a short period, one can only stand in awe of the magnitude of this achievement and the emergence of the state.

Look at former US secretary of state and academic Henry Kissinger, who could not offer any explanation for this great emergence of the state. But he hit the mark when he attributed it to the spiritual conviction instilled by the noble Prophet (PBUH) and the divine nature of the message.[84]

We present this presentation as indications of the spiritual dimension of the issue of the emergence of the state, and the three dimensions we have referred to are all interconnected, reinforcing each other, where necessity meets reason and the practical experimental requirements of life.

The theoretical and abstract nature of the concept of the emergence of the state in Islamic thought, as we have presented it, necessitates the definition of the content and methodology of the state.

[84] Henry Kissinger, *World Order* (Arab Book House, 2016), 101–103.

Through these, the state acquires its legitimacy and intellectual acceptance. However, before clarifying this content, it is necessary to address an important issue with a significant and widespread presence in our contemporary reality. This issue is often plagued by distorted views and misconceptions, and its dimensions are not confined to the realm of a few thinkers. Rather, it is addressed by the public, and many consider it fundamental and necessary within the context of shaping the content of the state. By this, I mean the widespread prevalence of what is known as "secularism," which sometimes takes other forms under the guise of a "civil state."

We must clarify, with precision, what we mean by "secularism" in both its partial and comprehensive senses. Partial secularism refers to the separation of religion from the state, while comprehensive secularism entails the separation of human values, ethics, and religion from public and private life.[85]

Partial secularism is a perspective on reality (procedural pragmatism) that does not concern itself with the broader dimensions of knowledge. It is confined to the realms of politics and economics, expressed by the separation of religion from the state. It does not provide any perspective on other areas of life, and therefore, it lacks any branches of a cognitive or ethical system. However, this partial perspective is a stage in the process of the emergence of secularism in its comprehensive sense.

Comprehensive secularism is a holistic perspective on existence with final cognitive dimensions that define the relationship between metaphysical principles and religion in all areas of life. It is a materialistic perspective within the framework of the reference to the unity of material/natural existence. It views the world as fundamentally composed of matter with no inherent sanctity, in a constant motion without purpose, and that it constitutes both man and nature. It is a one, natural, material vision in its becoming and movement, devoid of any connection to ethics or religion, and it does not know them at all. Its cognitive system originates from sensory perception and

---

[85] Abdul-Wahab al-Masiri, *Partial and Comprehensive Secularism* (Al-Shorouq Publishing House, 2002), 60.

material reality as the sole source of knowledge. The world given to our senses contains within it enough to be interpreted and dealt with. The ethical system is also based on materialistic knowledge as the sole source of ethics. Additionally, its historical perspective follows a single path, viewing humans as part of nature/material with no independent boundaries separating them. Therefore, it is a one-dimensional phenomenon. Comprehensive secularism goes beyond merely separating religion from the state, but it also separates all ethical, religious, and humanitarian values from public and private life.[86]

In researching the data that forms the background for this secular trend, we can indicate the following:

1. Practical experimental data.
2. Intellectual data related to the perspective of existence and divinity.

The practical experimental data stems from the rule of the church in Europe during the Middle Ages, its alliance with feudalism, and its approach that suppressed science and scientists. These are well-known facts to the public, and its history is filled with violence, persecution, and oppression. What's worse is the position of the Catholic religious institution and its grasp on power as an intermediary between man and his Lord.[87]

The other data is based on the Enlightenment era and the writings of Western thinkers (naturalists, positivists, materialists, etc.), whose ideas we discussed in chapter 2 of this study (the concept of humans). Despite the writings of some rationalist thinkers who acknowledge the existence of God (without revelation) or idealists and the Western intellectual trend in its early stages (Immanuel Kant, Descartes, Spinoza, etc.) who recognize the existence of God but deny revelation and put man as the reference for existence (the humanist trend), but they exclude God as a reference for the universe as they

---

[86] Abdul-Wahab al-Masiri, *Partial and Comprehensive Secularism*, 220–225.

[87] Muhammad Amara, *The Islamic State Between Secularism and Religious Authority* (Al-Shorouk Publishing House, 1988), 170.

exclude Him from any knowledge and from the process of formulating ethical systems. This is a stage in Western thought that ended with the predominance of the perspective of nature/material, as we explained above, which objectified the individual human searching for (benefit) and created it as a criterion for good and evil (the doctrine of pleasure and pain). The physical human being searching for his benefit and pleasure as an absolute good is met with pain as evil.

Accordingly, as we have indicated, all religious values, ethical systems, and value systems have been eliminated. This led Julien Offray de La Mettrie, the founder of the secularist school, to declare that everything in existence is subject to sensory perception and measurement, and anything beyond that has no existence.[88] This is the doctrine of nature/material, the reflections of which still exist among contemporary liberal thinkers. We have previously mentioned contemporary thinkers like Dewey and Professor Ayer, despite the vigorous attempts to confine Christianity within certain limits, to restore its credibility and to exclude it from political and economic life. Even though Pope Paul VI played an important international political role in the efforts to dismantle the socialist camp, especially in Poland. And despite the intellectual attempts to reconcile Christianity with secularism.[89]

Our critical view of the secular trend is based on scientific and logical analysis and certainly on deduction from Islamic thought, which we present below.

In the field of partial secularism, which involves the separation of religious institutions from state institutions, if it confines secularization to political, economic, administrative, and bureaucratic procedures, without encroaching on governing values and the ultimate reference point for society and the state, this separation exists in almost all human societies. Religious institutions cannot merge with political institutions in any political or civilizational framework. This

---

88 Roger Garaudy, *Contemporary Fundamentalisms: Their Causes and Manifestations* (Year 2000 Publishing House, 2000), 17–24.

89 Jurgen Habermas and Joseph Ratzinger (Pope Benedict XVI), *The Dialectics of Secularization: On Reason and Religion* (Jadawel Publishing and Distribution, 2013).

separation is widely accepted when it merely distinguishes political aspects from religious ones. Advocates of partial secularism within these boundaries assert that there is no inherent conflict between secularism in this context and religion; they can coexist. In this context, when the Prophet Muhammad (PBUH) said, "You are more knowledgeable about your worldly affairs," I believe it aligns with what we have mentioned above.

On the other hand, concerning Islam exclusively, it is not based on a hierarchical structure and bears no resemblance to the ecclesiastical order. Thus, the concept of religious institutions that existed in the Middle Ages under the rule of the church, acting as an intermediary between humans and their deities, is not applicable in Islamic doctrine. The relationship between humans and their Creator in Islam is direct, without hierarchical institutions or structures. Therefore, the traditional Western trajectory toward secularism has no relevance in the Islamic perspective, and Muslims do not need it. Secularism, as a characteristic, is specific to a certain European Catholic context in a specific historical period and cannot be universally applied.

Regarding the comprehensive perspective of secularism, as we have mentioned, it is based on the practical experimental datum and the datum of the perspective of existence and God. We see the following.

The practical experimental datum, when subjected to the methodology of induction to reach conclusions systematically and scientifically, is found to lack any scientifically documented basis in mathematical statistics. A single observation of a single variable within a specific period cannot provide a general result or judgment. For example, the single observation of a case of (church rule) as a single variable (Catholic) during a specific period (the Middle Ages) represents incomplete data that lead to invalid conclusions. Such conclusions cannot be considered truthful according to statistical mathematical analysis and measurement.[90]

---

90 The author is well-versed in this field and served as chief expert at the Arab Statistical Center for a long time.

This is in terms of quantitative, scientific, and mathematical analysis. Isn't this what experimentalists go for? Isn't that a scientific analysis that removes the status of the general rule inferred from the European Catholic case in the Middle Ages? Thus, it imposes the study of repeated cases in the world to reach a correct and honest extrapolation.

From another angle, how can they provide absolute rulings for the whole? Relativity remains within the limits of the presented case. It is not possible to reach absolute judgments through it except with a comprehensive theoretical vision, not with specific material data. This is evidence of the corruption of governance as secularism has adopted and the use of its rule in all times and places.

As for the criterion based on the vision of existence and the divine, the stance reached by this perspective, by negating religion, values systems, and ethical systems from public and private life, according to the material/nature reference as presented above, we see it as merely a trend of purely intellectual views that are subject to refutation. Indeed, they are susceptible to being refuted by thinkers (even liberals among them) in a postmodern stage, and their attack on the notion of disconnecting from everything metaphysical and from all the heritage of the pre-Enlightenment era. As for Islamic thought, we have previously clarified its perspective that revelation is divine enlightenment defined in aspects of human life and behavior, both individual and collective, while leaving room for the broad domain of applied and experimental sciences of reason. It unequivocally denies any conflict between revelation and reason, making it imperative for every Muslim to seek knowledge.

From this standpoint, whether from the data of practical experience or the intellectual implications of Islamic thought, we see in comprehensive secularism a position lacking in authenticity in its reasoning, stripping humanity of the essence of its spirit based on virtue and creating a materialistic human being, relentlessly pursuing the satisfaction of their material and physical desires.

The Islamic belief in continuous evolution and the broad space granted to reason (intellectual independence) in reaching practical laws and judgments within the context of societal development and lifestyle patterns, as reflected by real-life experiences and the requirements of progress and advancement, has led to an approach in which the form of the state emanates from a synthesis of intellect, revelation, wisdom, Sharia, worldly matters, and the afterlife. This approach, derived from the spirit of Islam, as we see it, makes Islam not specify a particular form for the system of governance,[91] but rather, it confines the specification to the imam/caliph at the head of the state.

[The placement between two brackets is intended and will be explained below.]

It is very clear that Islam did not limit its address to the individual conscience and did not limit itself to the spiritual dimension only. It carries in its data all the dimensions of the comprehensive approach to earthly existence and lifestyles, all the way to the otherworldly dimensions, and according to the contexts of reason and transmission, revelation is divine enlightenment, and reason is the ability and possibility of human excellence to reach the state that characterizes his best evaluation, whether in the face of the requirements of worldly life or what divine enlightenment has brought, which makes it impossible for there to be a contradiction between law and reason, as we indicated previously.

Therefore, defining the form of governance represents open-ended processes of evolution. The variation among Islamic schools of thought, particularly in the formulation of leadership, is not the focus of this study, nor is it within its scope to delve into a historical investigation of imamate and caliphate. Thus, in the twenty-first century, drawing from the spirit of Islam with a grounding based on Islamic thought and contemporary realities and rational judgments, the spirit of objectives aims to maintain consistency between divine enlightenment and the requirements of reason and empirical evidence. Consequently, the form of the state embodies both the principles of Sharia and practical wisdom. It can serve as a preventive management mechanism to safeguard and ensure spiritual dimensions, such as the concept of guardianship by a qualified jurist, based

[91] Muhammad Mahdi Shams al-Din, *The System of Governance and Administration in Islam* (University Institution for Studies, Publishing and Distribution, 1991).

on the specifications outlined in Islamic jurisprudence references. This is achieved through mechanisms and processes where the nation plays an affirmative role (i.e., self-governance), essentially reflecting a system of governance that aligns with the times and allows the people to endorse governance institutions. This is coupled with a high level of scientific competence, directing pathways that prevent deviation from divine enlightenment while preserving the nation's decision-making autonomy and adhering to rational judgments. The hallmark of governance in such a system is based on justice, preserving the value system and moral framework and enabling their application in both public and private life.

Chapter 5

The Concept of Ethics

Economics is an ethical science, not only in the sense that it addresses the material and spiritual requirements of life in its entirety but also in the practical dimensions of its vocabulary (such as interest, prices, monopolies, consumer behavior, etc.), where ethics serves as a standard for evaluating actions as either good or bad. It emphasizes the necessity of rationality, meaning that ethics are applied practically. Moreover, in broader contexts, ethics serve as a comprehensive standard based on a theory with rational or faith-based extensions, thus becoming normative ethics. For example, the ethical stance on issues like murder or the moral values of truthfulness and lying represent higher ethical principles.

From this perspective, it becomes a legitimate question to inquire about the source of ethics: the mind, transportation, nature, and the secretions of public life! Is it absolute for all times and places, or is it a product of the environment governed by the prevailing social conditions in a specific time and place?

Ethics, in its relationship to economics, has become a fundamental pillar as a standard for the economic perspective. It serves not only as a starting point for understanding phenomena but also as a method for dealing with these phenomena to achieve the best possible outcome. In this sense, it becomes a necessity in economic studies.

The varied views on the source, universality, and foundations of ethics have made it one of the most crucial subjects addressed by philosophical thought as a background for economic thought. These views are based on a comprehensive existential perspective of the relationship between humans and the Creator, the self, the other, society, and nature. It is what we aim to address in our study. Our focus is not on ethics as specific rules for specific behaviors but rather on ethics as a perspective within theoretical wisdom (the philosophy of ethics) and the extent to which it is reflected or adhered to within practical reality.

Ethical values are independent of the individuals who adhere to them, and they are subject to variations in perspectives, as we have indicated. Therefore, our approach will involve discussing the perspectives of Western thinkers (whether currents, schools, or specific thinkers), and its presentation will precede our presentation of Islamic thought and perspective on ethics, focusing on relatively modern schools due to the impossibility of discussing this scope comprehensively, given its historical dimensions, which require extensive and in-depth study reaching into the depths of human thought since the dawn of humanity. For the same reasons that led us to discuss Western liberal thought, as mentioned earlier, we will confine the presentation and discussion to the most prominent intellectual propositions of Western liberal thought:

- The doctrine of utilitarianism or, in other words, the doctrine of ethical consequences, which goes to the best consequences holds that the morally right action is the one that produces a greater amount of utility or benefit. Actions that benefit or harm someone are the only ones that can be deemed right or wrong.[92] This doctrine is strongly associated with Jeremy Bentham (1748–1832) and John Stuart Mill (1806–1873). Its roots in philosophy can be traced back to the ancient Greek Epicureans, where the philosopher Aristippus argued that pleasure is the voice of nature and instinct is the primary motive for human actions. The criterion for measuring the goodness or badness of actions

[92] Julian Baggini, *Philosophy*, 110.

is the balance between pleasure and pain. As empirical tendencies flourished in the modern era, the utilitarian doctrine attempted to redefine the principle of pleasure with the intervention of thought to regulate pleasures.[93] Thus, they replaced the concept of "pleasure" and "happiness" with another concept based on considering the interests of humanity rather than focusing solely on the individual's well-being. "Utility," for them, took a social character (the welfare of all), and their doctrine was termed "ethics of general utility."[94]

- Bentham argued that people naturally seek pleasure and avoid pain, but what distinguishes them from animals is their use of reason when following the principle of utility. Therefore, since reason governs what is good, Bentham saw goodness as resulting in pleasure, opposite to actions leading to increased pain. Thus, actions are judged by their consequences rather than intentions and motives. This experimental view of the utilitarian school evaluates "good" based on empirical evidence, which is the pathway to prove what is desired by people. Attempting to extend this concept to society without restricting it to individuals, Bentham posited that what is beneficial for us is also beneficial for others, thus personal utility is linked to general utility. The key is the quantity of pleasure as the aim is to include the maximum number of individuals experiencing pleasure. Hence, Bentham viewed utilitarianism as revolving around the principle of maximizing happiness for the greatest number of people, disregarding motives or intentions and focusing solely on outcomes or facts.
- John Stuart Mill followed a similar path to Bentham in his treatment of ethics, making it science and descriptive, whose subject is describing the behavior of individuals in society. Therefore, research on its subject, ethics, is neces-

---

93 Mustafa Hilmi, *Ethics* (www.kotobarabia), 59–60.

94 Zakaria Ibrahim, *The Moral Problem* (Library of Egypt), 147–148.

sarily inductive and experimental. In essence, it is the same similarity between Bentham and Mill, with some formal modifications that we will mention. Even after the critical influence of hedonism, under the title of virtue, Mill still adhered even to its terminology. In his work *Utilitarianism*, he stated: "Those who desire virtue for its own sake desire it either because the consciousness of it is a pleasure, or because the consciousness of being without it is a pain or for both reasons combined…" And he also states that "happiness is the sole end of human action, and the promotion of it is the test by which to judge all human conduct. Hence, the standard by which morality must be judged is as long as it is contained within the whole."[95] In another part of the same book, he wrote: "The principle of utility, or the greatest happiness principle, holds that actions are right in proportion as they tend to promote happiness, wrong as they tend to produce the reverse of happiness."[96] Happiness being pleasure and its opposite being pain.

The two modifications we mentioned are the result of criticism directed toward utilitarianism and under the influence of German idealism, especially Kant and Hegel:

1) Pleasure is not entirely reducible to sensory pleasure, as Bentham saw it. There is also a moral pleasure connected to the higher functions of human life, which is nobler than the functions of worldly life.
2) Subordination of individual utility to collective utility, according to the theological principles of loving your neighbor as yourself. Mill, influenced by these modifications, stated, "The good is what is aimed at by the wise and cherished by the rational man."[97]

---

[95] John Stuart Mill, *Utilitarianism* (Center for Arab Unity Studies, 2012), 82–83.

[96] Ibid., 37.

[97] Mustafa Hilmi, *Ethics*, 65. From Dr. Tawfiq Al-Taweel, *Moral Philosophy* (Dar Al-Nahda Al-Arabiya, 1967), 269–270.

Situational ethics

The field of ethics relies on their experimental philosophy according to the inductive method. Thus, their perspective on ethics comes from studying the prevalent customs and traditions in society based on observation. Therefore, this perspective has become a branch of sociology as a realistic experimental science, denying the role of human conscience and intellect and transcending the relativity of time and place. (The founder of situational theory—Auguste Comte 1581.)

The doctrine of utilitarianism, or the duty doctrine, as proposed by Immanuel Kant (which we will discuss later), was not accepted. The first acknowledges the influence and denies the inherent variability in human nature, while the second is based on metaphysical foundations that cannot be explored through empirical scientific methods. Therefore, ethics are seen as based on situational knowledge and realize its qualities, making ethics relative rather than absolute. But more importantly, our topic is what was presented in the logical positivist philosophy of situationism, as articulated by modern thinkers like Carnap and Professor Ayer, who not only denied the absolute nature of ethics but also denied the existence of "ethical issues" altogether.

In Carnap's ethical philosophy, there is no investigation into facts. Rather, it is a supposed inquiry into what is good and what is bad—that is, what actions are permissible and what actions are not, based on logical issues. These are fictitious issues that do not express anything verifiable empirically. Ethical judgments, according to Carnap, are nothing but expressions of certain emotions or reactions."[98]

According to logical positivism, any proposition is considered meaningless unless it can be verified empirically. For example, if we say "eternal and infinite God," this is a judgment that cannot be verified empirically and thus is merely a linguistic expression that cannot be judged as true or false. Therefore, logical positivists deny not only ethical judgments but also all metaphysical and spiritual aspects of rational judgments.

---

[98] Zakaria Ibrahim, *The Moral Problem*, 68.

Immanuel Kant's ethical philosophy

The most prominent thinker in Western thought presents refutations of the utilitarian perspective as the criterion and basis for ethical theory. In his works (such as *Critique of Pure Reason*, *Critique of Practical Reason*, and *Build the Metaphysics of Morals*), he discusses a theory of ethics centered on "duty" based on goodwill. According to Kant, morally good actions reside in intentions, not consequences. Goodwill is the only thing that can be considered intrinsically good as its goodness is not derived from the goals it achieves or the goals it seeks but as a necessary and sufficient condition for all morality. All its effects derive its goodness from the core of its structure. The concept of goodwill entails a duty that the agent must fulfill. This duty is based on the formal principle of will and is not influenced by personal desires, whims, or materialistic goals. Such desires and goals are products of human desires and are therefore not absolute or necessary. Creative actions must always be universal and applicable in all places. They must necessarily conform to a general law that is the absolute support for all ethics.[99]

Moral conceptions cannot be derived from any empirical knowledge. They are therefore speculative knowledge, and in the clarity of their approach lies their merit, making them suitable to be the highest practical principles that guide our actions. Each time we add an empirical element to them, we diminish their original impact to the same extent, stripping actions of their absolute value. This necessity is not limited to theoretical considerations alone when we engage in pure contemplation. Rather, from a practical standpoint, these conceptions and laws must be drawn from the pure source of action and presented in their purest form, uncontaminated by anything else. Furthermore, we determine the extent of this practical intellectual knowledge, which is nonetheless pure knowledge.[100] Thus, Kant finds that pure empiricism is an enemy of ethics because it negates

[99] Ibid., 163–171.

[100] Immanuel Kant, *Foundations of Metaphysics of Morals* (National Printing and Publishing House, 1965), 47.

or denies all objective certainty as well as doubts the existence of first principles independent of experience.

Therefore, Kant identifies the main characteristics of ethics of duty or obligation as follows:

1) Duty is purely formal, meaning it is legislation or a comprehensive rule unrelated to changes in experience. Duty and pure reason are the same.
2) Duty is devoid of purpose; it does not seek to achieve utility or attain happiness but is sought for its own sake.
3) Duty is an unconditional principle for action, meaning that duty is a law that precedes any empirical conception; therefore, it is absolute, necessary, and unconditional.[101]

If human will is a mixture of sensation and reason, it may conceive of good, or it may resort to committing evil. When subjected to sensory motives, it may conflict with action or with laws. Therefore, this will must have "binding commands" that compel it to do what reason deems good. Here, Kant denies any role or need for divine will, considering that this will can renew itself and make its decisions once it conceives of good according to what moral law dictates rationally.[102]

On the other hand, Kant argues that this moral duty returns to the idea of God Almighty, who endowed us with reason and entrusted in it the fundamental truths, including ethical truths. In other words, the independent rational principles owe their existence to the Creator.

Here we must point out a fundamental issue in Kant's thought, which makes the moral evidence based on absolute will a derivative of the self, and the concept of God is derived from it or formulated from it. It is not the other way around; thus, ethics descends from the level of religion, just as humans descend from the level of the divine.[103]

---

[101] Zakaria Ibrahim, *The Moral Problem*, 167–171.

[102] Ibid., 171–172.

[103] Idris Hani, *Our Ethics in Need of an Alternative Moral Philosophy* (Civilization Center for the Development of Islamic Thought, 2009), 33.

The Islamic perspective for ethics

The foundation of the Islamic message lies in the impact on practical life, in a way that it becomes a standard for effectiveness and a methodology for elevating human beings toward nobility and perfection. This is the supreme goal of the prophetic mission: "I was only sent to perfect noble character," as emphasized by the noble Prophet. These noble character traits are embodied manifestations of the religion, which is the religion of interaction.

In the Islamic perspective, ethics are classified under the terms "goodness" and "ugliness" of actions. The initiation or avoidance of actions is based on the motive of virtue as a determinant for the human soul, which is governed by two forces: the force of desire and the force of reason. The first pertains to bodily desires and pleasures, while the second seeks elevation, knowledge, beauty, and ugliness. In the Islamic view, there are two rational principles: the intellect recognizes inherently the goodness and ugliness of things without reference to religious law. Every rational person affirms the goodness of good actions, praises them, and disapproves of bad actions, condemning them. These judgments are necessary and indisputable, not derived from religious law as asserted by the rationalists and atheists without acknowledging the divine law, as mentioned by Nasir al-Din al-Tusi in his work *The Summation of Belief*. Based on this approach, actions are classified according to their goodness or ugliness, where goodness entails actions that are not subject to condemnation, while ugliness entails the opposite. Therefore, the judgment of reason is as follows.

The action that neither deserves praise nor blame for doing it or leaving it is the "permissible" action. The action deserving praise for doing it and blame for leaving it is the "obligatory" action. The action deserving praise for doing it but not blame for leaving it is the "recommended" action. The action deserving praise for leaving it but not blame for doing it is the "disliked" action. Of course, there is also the forbidden (haram) action, whether by rational judgment or by religious law, legal code, or conscience.

However, in the Islamic message and its paths of divine guidance, there must be the inclusion of "divine enlightenment" to support the intellect. This is because human rational principles vary in scientific possibility, knowledge, and mental perception, leading to contradictory social judgments. There are necessities in various situations for a comprehensive framework that outlines public life strategies. Hence, the noble prophetic mission encapsulates the Islamic perspective on the relationship between divine law and reason, acknowledging their complementarity in determining the path of virtue toward human perfection.

Furthermore, divine law is necessary for elucidating the correctness of the approach, granting legitimacy to punishment and reward.

From the Islamic perspective, the intrinsic motive of human conduct isn't solely contingent upon outcomes, despite their significance; rather, it's not a precondition. The condition for virtuous action is anchored in intentions aimed at benefiting people. Thus, ethics emerge as clear indicators of intentions.

In the context of human behavior and relationships with others and society, ethics hold a position that surpasses even religious rituals. While religious rituals are prescribed and defined, with the abandonment of them as deserving punishment, acts of virtue occupy a higher status as they are considered acts of supererogation and grace. Therefore, we see that religious rituals inherently contain motives for ethical behavior, as indicated by this verse: "Prayer prohibits immorality and wrongdoing."[104]

Within this context, the field of human behavior and individual and group relations comes from the hadith of Imam Ali (PBUH) in *Nahj al-Balagha*, referred to previously: "Do not ask about their prayers, their fasting, their frequent pilgrimages, and their humming at night. Ask about their good deeds and the fulfillment of their trusts."

The practical implications and methodology of instilling ethical values in society, particularly in Islamic thought, manifest in the concepts of enjoining good and forbidding evil as a means of guiding human behavior. This rises to the level of conditional obligation,

---

[104] Surah Al-Ankabut, verse 45.

requiring action through speech, action, and intention. The conditions for this obligation are as follows:

1) The one who initiates the action knows the command and prohibition rationally and legally, so what is good is known and what is evil is evil.
2) It is obligatory to influence the action, and if there is no ability to influence, the obligation is invalid.
3) Absence of corruption. If the perpetrator knew or thought it most likely that corruption would occur for him or some others in his command and prohibition, the obligation would be waived.[105]

From this comprehensive perspective, the partial standard rules branch out, where we find a vast amount in Islamic literature of directives and prohibitions for doing good and avoiding evil. This vast amount constitutes indirect formulations of the details of divine kindness in enlightening humanity. For example, in *Principles of Al-Kafi* Volume 2 by Al-Kulayni,[106] we find comprehensive chapters covering various aspects of human behavior, all based on the principle of enjoining good and forbidding evil in their practical realizations.

---

[105] Nasir al-Din Muhammad ibn Hasan al-Tusi, *The Disclosure of the Intended in Abstracting Belief*, 406–407.

[106] Al-Kulayni, *Principles of Al-Kafi*, vol. 2.

Chapter 6

Justice

The system of moral values takes precedence as a central and normative value for all dimensions of social, material, and spiritual life. It has been reported by Imam Ali (Q) in *Nahj al-Balagha* that "justice puts things in their places," implying that every matter has a specific position dictated either by reason, Sharia, or other principles like natural law or general welfare in the cosmic order and so forth. The criterion of justice serves as a source of legitimacy for beliefs, thoughts, actions, and the correctness of relationships between individuals, communities, and governance. Justice extends beyond human existence to govern the relationship between the Creator and the created beings, addressing divine justice, human free will, fate, and rewards and punishments. Justice may take absolute values in the structure of belief, and its normativity is exercised in practical and procedural wisdom, whether in legislation and the judiciary, in the fairness of the distribution of wealth or partial relative facts in the approach to practicing life and its development and so on. Thus, justice established a balanced and accurate assessment of matters.

If the concept of justice was presented in terms that expressed the background of thought that dealt with such (justice is fairness, justice is an entitlement, justice is giving everyone his right, and so forth), then the source of justice, its priority, and its overall scope was the subject of disagreement in the context of intellectual schools of thought and in our research here, which focuses on economic thought and its philosophical background. We find ourselves presenting the concept of justice in its absolute scope and its differences in liberal thought, as was done in the context of research in other places, followed by the content of Islamic thought in its philosophical background and overall contexts, while excluding partial concepts of justice and pointing out the importance of distributive justice because of its connection to our basic topic.

But this will certainly be stated in more detail in the other parts of the study. For justice to take its scope as a criterion for legitimacy, there must be laws to which individuals, society, and the state are subject. The sources of these laws differ according to the thought that formulates them, in addition to other determinants in the relationship between justice or right and the good, between the individual and the group, between the motive and the results, meaning the starting mechanism and the resulting outcome, and so on.

The contexts of liberal thought, although centered on individualism and united in their perspective on it, nevertheless differ in the perspective of justice and the source of the laws that determine its legitimacy. We refer here to the most prominent differing theories within liberal thought regarding the source of justice and its laws:

1) *Positivist theory.* This theory asserts that the state is authorized to use force to uphold its laws, and positivist law is deemed if it is sanctioned by the state based on its specific circumstances and the ruler's perspective.
2) *Natural law theory.* This theory recognizes laws that are accepted by reason and logic, and justice is measured according to its conformity to natural law.
3) *Utilitarian theory.* This theory sees justice as determined by the outcomes that lead to individual benefit and the greatest good for the greatest number of individuals. While utilitarian theory has gained the greatest popularity in liberal thought and still has a contemporary presence today, the liberal thinker Immanuel Kant diverged from it according to his intellectual concept and the same motivations we mentioned in the context of ethics. However,

the most prominent figure in our contemporary setting is the achievement of the contemporary thinker John Rawls, who issued his famous book *A Theory of Justice* in 1971, followed by a new formulation entitled *Justice as Fairness*, thus opposing the utilitarian theory from the perspective of the social contract and with a different approach while drawing on the views of Immanuel Kant. Therefore, here we will only present the utilitarian theory followed by an overview of Rawls's thought, with references to Immanuel as required by the presentation.

The utilitarian theory, which emerged with the writings of David Hume and Jeremy Bentham, found its most prominent successor through John Stuart Mill, who defined its basic context as follows:

> There must be a standard by which we distinguish between good and evil, between the absolute and the relative, between ends and means, and whatever this standard may be, it can only be one standard… This general standard, according to which all rules of practical conduct should be tried, and which is considered as the test of their correctness, is the amount of happiness produced for the human race.
>
> And justice based on utility is the chief part, without dispute, the most sacred and the most obligatory part of all ethics.[107]

Despite the occasional perceived conflict between utility and considerations of justice, where prioritizing utility often leads to justifying injustice, there are numerous practical examples in this context. Nevertheless, the utilitarian doctrine rejects this contradiction between utility and justice. Rather, justice has no explanation

[107] John Stuart Mill, *Utilitarianism*, 87–120.

except in terms of utilitarian principles, as John Stuart Mill argues. Therefore, considerations of utility dictate that justice is derived from utility itself and is not an independent principle.

As a counterpoint to the utilitarian perspective, liberalism emerges in a context where ideas of justice and individual rights play a central role. It embodies a "duty ethics" liberalism, as articulated by Immanuel Kant, where priority is given to justice in ethical values. Justice carries a direct moral meaning. It is not merely a value to be weighed according to situational demands, but it is the highest social virtue. Thus, if achieving human happiness is possible through unjust means, then justice, not happiness, should prevail. When issues are framed from the perspective of justice in certain individual rights, the common good itself cannot transcend these rights.[108] The principles of right are derived independently of goodness, and right, as it is independent, restricts goodness and defines its limits for it. So the ethics of duty theory is opposed to the utilitarian perspective in terms of teleology, meaning actions with their conclusions "results matter."

The foundation of law, as we mentioned in the previous paragraph regarding ethical law, lies within the general reason, not in its subject matter. It resides within an entity capable of independent will, not merely as an experimental end but as an entity with purposes: precedence over its subjects and independent from them. If rights precede the good, then the self precedes its ends.

The transcendent self, which precedes any experience, provides the conceptual framework for the law that governs actions. Thus, the epistemic authority of the self transitions to practical authority as a rational agent.

Contemporary thinker John Rawls published his book *A Theory of Justice* in 1971 and followed it with amendments in his book *Justice as Fairness*. In the spirit of his book, Rawls is considered a liberal who believes in the morality of duty and supports his propositions with the data of Immanuel Kant, but he proposes formulas that differ from Kant when he puts the contexts of justice within perspective.

---

[108] Michael J. Sandel, *Liberalism and the Limits of Justice* (Center for Arab Unity Studies, 2009), 35–50.

Practical. Rawls decides that justice is the first virtue and presents his theory, which is a revival of the theory of the social contract (Hobbes, Locke, Rousseau) and has been mixed with the rational nature of Immanuel Kant, in which justice is the basis of the social structure, so all legislative and political procedures must be coordinated with what it stipulates. It contains the principles of justice based on the distribution of good things (money, prestige, freedom, opportunities, self-respect, and so forth) and thus creates basic principles as starting points for justice:

- The principle of the free individual enjoying the right to life, the right to freedom, and the property right.
- Public reason that produces public law according to the five formulas mentioned by Immanuel Kant in the absolute moral imperative:

    1) Work only according to your law.
    2) Work as if the law of your self-employment will become a general law.
    3) Work so that humanity in your person is an end, as it is in every other person, and not a means.
    4) Act with your will so that it creates a general law through its law.
    5) Work as if you were a member of the Kingdom of Public Goals project.

- The principle of "legitimate member of the kingdom of ends" through the original position in the veil of ignorance. (We will explain that.)
- The contract is hypothetical, not realistic.
- Obedience on the part of the citizen who has accepted the social contract and must obey its provisions (a church idea).[109]

[109] John Rawls, *Justice as Fairness* (Center for Arab Unity Studies, 2009), 41–42.

The legislators in Rawls's theory are a group of individuals who possess extensive knowledge in various fields, but they do not know their own identity (the veil of ignorance). It is done to impart objectivity in their approach to legislation. They are the ones who decide on the terms of the social contract, which Rawls refers to as the "original position." Consequently, the negotiators, who have absolute freedom in reviewing the principles of justice and its dimensions, will objectively determine the state of justice manifested in its perfection. Only one condition related to "equality" will have an exception, where it will be beneficial to the utmost extent for those with the least advantages.[110]

Through this, we see Rawls's strong focus on rational foundations in his comparison between principles to achieve what is acceptable and binding for humans. This context resonates with the church's approach to reaching the "absolute moral imperative."

In our presentation of justice in Islamic thought, it must be noted that we will not delve into the differences between Islamic sects but rather present the most complete scenario that satisfies the author's conviction. We also point out the approach to dealing with this thought, which is based on deduction and inference. As for the context of the inductive approach, the author's conviction is that Islamic systems historically, except during the initial period of revelation, did not fully reflect Islamic thought in its ideal form. Instead, they were subjected to adaptation according to the dictates of the political situation, driven by the interests of rulers. Nevertheless, we can arrive at judgments at a partial level that express Islamic thought.

Justice is one of the fundamental principles of the Islamic religion, encompassing dimensions such as divine justice in cosmic existence, predestination, human free will, and the issue of reward and punishment. It extends to its implications in integration with justice among humans in the relationship between individuals, society, and governance. In Islamic thought, justice encompasses the concept of moral excellence and ugliness in actions, serving as a criterion for

[110] Anthony de Crespin and Kenneth Minogue, *Figures of Contemporary Political Philosophy* (Egyptian Book Authority, 1996), 138–144.

determining the goodness or ugliness of actions based on rational perception. It is the reason capable of discerning between the ugliness or goodness of actions.

In the same context as the ethical framework, which reinforces the intellect and is based on the same premises regarding the variation in intellectual capacities, Sharia law comes to shape the reflective state of divine justice, supporting reason in a complementary formula devoid of any contradictory state or phenomenon carrying the meaning of contradiction. It resorts to interpreting Sharia law in a manner consistent with reason, as mentioned earlier.

Reason can distinguish between goodness and ugliness to describe an action based on the standard of justice. Without intellectual judgment, Sharia law would not be established. If we do not acknowledge intellectual judgment of goodness and ugliness, there would be no confirmation of Sharia law among divine laws. It would be possible for a liar to claim miracles, and there is no evidence to refute this possibility, so there is no certainty in the truthfulness of his claim.[111]

According to this context, the definition of justice, as stated by Imam Ali (PBUH), is that "justice places things in their rightful positions," as mentioned in *Nahj al-Balagha* (section of governance). This means that everything has its rightful place, either determined by reason or by religious law and the general interests in the system of the universe. Justice is about preserving that order and avoiding deviation toward excess or negligence.[112]

The Quranic verse goes: "Indeed, we sent Our messengers with clear proofs, and We sent down with them the Scripture and the balance that the people may maintain [their affairs] in justice."[113]

Achieving justice on earth is based on human action. Free human will, based on its judgments, on the balance between the interests of individuals and the public interest.

---

[111] Jaafar al-Sabhani, *Concepts of the Quran* (Al Bayt Foundation for the Revival of Heritage), 16.

[112] Ibid., 19.

[113] Surah Al-Hadid, verse 25.

The fundamental criterion in the context of fair governance is based on preventing injustice and adhering to the principle of "no harm and no reciprocating harm. It is better to prevent harm than to bring benefit, especially if the harm is general." This principle is based on promoting public welfare that negates any unjust action or harm to society resulting from individual rights.

"Indeed, Allah orders justice and good conduct and giving to relatives and forbids immorality and bad conduct, and oppression. He admonishes you that perhaps you will be reminded."[114]

What we have presented constitutes fundamental principles for initiating fair judgments at a practical level, where Islamic thought is rich in its partial and relative positions. Whether it's distributive justice, justice in interpersonal relationships, justice in governance, and so on, Sharia delves into its details, just as intellectual reasoning does in its judgments. It addresses judgments under various headings such as transactions, contracts, penalties, and policies, with open avenues for interpretation to deal with new developments under the title "Changing Judgments with Time and Place."

[114] Surah Al-Nahl, verse 90.

Part 2

Economic Doctrine

Introduction

The existence of what is actual and present in our era is the same as in all eras. Matters and objects' existence are either not by our choice and action or the result of our choice and action.[115] Cognitive awareness of the movement and becoming of things according to universal scientific laws, characterized by relative absoluteness, requires presence. The rational senses perceive the external formation of beings, and the mind, with its perceptions, dives into the essence of the formation and inner movement of beings. From this standpoint, the theoretical vision of "theoretical wisdom" is determined, which is the completion of the soul by learning and encompassing knowledge of the starting points of things in their existence, a knowledge that puts the practical perspective of "practical wisdom" as knowledge of an opinion in action, on the correct and truthful basis in the opinion embodied through this theoretical perspective. The external existence of things results in its effects and rulings, and the mental perception does not result in its effects and rulings, and our knowledge of everything is an expression of the attainment of the essence of things in our souls stripped of their external materials.[116]

Here, "knowledge" of things consists of their external beings and their psychological qualities. Knowledge of essence is essence and knowledge of attributes is attributes. Due to the difficulty of these forms, some have denied the mental existence of things.[117] Thus, the contrast in principle forms the basis for seeing the existence and movement of things.

---

[115] Ibn Sina, *The Metaphysics of the Healing*, 6.

[116] Ibid., 569.

[117] Ibid.

In the subject of existence that we addressed in the first chapter of this work, views on the Creator varied from denial of His existence to recognition of Him detached from revelation and to the Islamic perspective, which considers revelation as divine enlightenment. These views reflect an understanding of the relationship between nature, humanity, and the occurrence of action and how it relates to human behavior. It leads to a perspective in cognitive development—namely, the extent of knowledge of a thing as theoretical wisdom and its impact on action as practical wisdom. Consequently, variations arise in the interpretation of reality and the economic movement in the interpretation of phenomena, judgments, and theories as this is reflected in the sources of knowledge.

Methods of knowledge vary between scientific proof (purely rational research), revelation (knowledge), and denial or approval of transmission as this latter perspective of transmission comes in a complementary position with reason, meaning that reason alone cannot achieve certainty unless it is illuminated by the light of Sharia and the support of reason. Political economy is one of the branches of the human sciences concerned with "the study of humanity in the practice of its ordinary life affairs."

As the economic teacher Marshall says, the human sciences, including the science of economics, are distinguished from the applied natural sciences, whether in approach or methodology in investigating phenomena or in the intellectual perspective of the researcher. In the field of human sciences, beliefs, ideology, and cosmic vision play a significant role, unlike in natural phenomena where there is no will or choice and causes are specific and limited. Consequently, researchers in natural phenomena strive to uncover truth without the influence of doctrines and ideology. On the other hand, in human sciences, researchers often impose their beliefs and opinions on the interpretation of phenomena.

In that regard, the context of research in economics took the following directions, according to what was stated by the economic thinker Joseph Schumpeter (1883–1950) in his great book *The History of Economic Analysis*:

1) The economic doctrine that comes closer to the meaning of doctrine, principles, and standards than it suggests an analysis of phenomena with a quantitative, material existence.
2) Economic theory or economic analysis of phenomena, their mutual influence, causality, and finality, which formulates general laws governing economic relations, and is close in its approach to the methods of the natural sciences, whether in its mathematical analysis, use of statistics, or subjecting it to the correlation of its results with material reality.
3) Economic policies or applied measures inspired by prevailing ideas at the time and often expressing specific authoritarian interests.

Based on that, in the context of our work, we will review the emergence and formation of the classical liberal economic doctrine, with its philosophical intellectual background that we discussed in the first part of this work. Following this, we will undertake a conceptual endeavor based on deduction, measurement, and inference from Islamic thought sources, its fundamental references, and notable intellectual endeavors, aiming to establish an Islamic economic doctrine that is compatible with the realities of the time and deeply rooted in intellectual foundations. The themes of theory and judgments will be addressed in the third part of this work.

Chapter 7

Framework of Economic Doctrine

The economic doctrine considers beliefs and standard rules and adopts a perspective based on non-situational analytical foundations. Therefore, its comprehensive framework is characterized by totality, abstraction, and generality. It is not concerned with analyzing partial and relative phenomena except to the extent determined by its perspective and basis. In other words, it involves forming a specific theoretical vision for the practical analysis paths of materially existing phenomena, whether in their causality, the impact of their components, or the interpretation of their outcomes and potential implications. According to specific criteria, deviation from these criteria constitutes a reason to reject any judgment or conclusion reached. These criteria are binding standards for the correctness of the approach in any perspective of phenomena under analysis, from the viewpoint of the concerned economic doctrine.

The history of liberal economic thought with its recorded sources, the context of which we will discuss within the limits of this work, of course, not in a comprehensive manner but rather within the direct topics related to the propositions and objectives of our study, and these sources refer to the backgrounds of forming economic doctrine with philosophical dimensions, beliefs, and even expressions in an intellectual context that serves the interests of human groups in particular. This intellectual system intertwined beliefs with the efforts of thinkers that did not crystallize all at once on a specific date but instead took an evolutionary context whose inputs are still open to the present. It also included differences in visions of the efforts of thinkers, even within one doctrine, without deviating from the determinants of the main institution. Therefore, the doctrine was not defined by a comprehensive document but rather it was a crucible of schools of thought, individual thinkers, missionaries, philosophers, and theological visions of a religious trend.

According to the context that we have defined in this study, our work will remain confined within the framework of liberal thought and perspective due to its prevalence that guides most countries of the world, although in varying degrees, and its responsibility for policies that constitute the challenges of the era. Following this, we will attempt to form an Islamic economic doctrine that provides enlightenment for a deep vision in confronting contemporary challenges, serving as a renewed thought at the universal abstract level.

To grasp the influential and effective components of the economic doctrine, we will follow a methodology that defines the frameworks of the doctrine within the following axes:

- Ideology
- Theology
- The tool
- Performance mechanism

In the same context in which we address the liberal economic doctrine within these axes, we will also adopt it as a methodology in dealing with the establishment of an Islamic economic doctrine—of course, not out of similarity but rather as a scientific method in classifying thought according to its influential dimensions despite the sharp divergence in the intellectual formation and foundations.

Chapter 8

The Liberal Economic Doctrine

Liberal capitalist thought has evolved over centuries, with its chapters remaining open to new ideas and interpretations even in our contemporary era. It is the result of contributions from various economic schools of thought as well as individual works by philosophers and economic thinkers. This has led to the presence of different and sometimes conflicting proposals within the framework of liberal capitalist thought. In other words, the foundations and principles of this approach are not an approved document that is treated as a collective term that defines the frameworks of this doctrine as determinants of the classification of thought, its direction, and its rulings; but the context of emergence and crystallization has created distances over which liberal economic thinkers might meet, and they are almost the foundations of this doctrine that reach the limits of postulates. We may find the roots of this movement extending to Greek philosophy (since the fifth century BC), although the development of this doctrine began with its clear formation with the classical situation. The first was in the eighteenth century AD, and accordingly, in our demonstration of this doctrine, we present a vision of its foundations and principles in their broad outlines as pillars for this doctrine while reviewing, as much as possible, the schools and economic thinkers who contributed in the emergence and intellectual development of this doctrine, leaving the analysis of their economic theories to the third part of this book.

The foundations and principles of the liberal capitalist doctrine revolve around the following pillars:

1. Ideology. It is based on the following foundations:

Natural law. One of the most important foundations of liberal capitalist thought, which means the set of rules that nature imposes on all animals (of course, including humans). This law goes back to its roots in Greek thought before Christ and took its clearest extension at the hands of the Scholastics in the fifteenth century, then developed in its economic dimension with classical capitalist philosophers and thinkers in the eighteenth century, and it still has an active presence in our contemporary era through neoliberal thought.

In Aristotle's view, "natural" takes on a narrow meaning, referring to the forms of behavior imposed by the general necessities of life itself, which humans share with other animals.[118]

The Romans gave natural law a legal dimension by adapting it to fit social life through positive law (human law) in the official Roman sense. This is represented by necessity derived from natural law or by adapting its principles to suit specific circumstances. Any legislation that violates any rule of natural law is not considered legitimate law.[119]

The Scholastics, led by Thomas Aquinas, introduced what can be called the Aquinas theory of natural and positive law. Natural law is a just law. What is naturally just is represented by what is binding on us according to the nature of the situation, which means the relationship of this law to human rights, because natural law, according to the Scholastics, is considered a source of rules. The applicable law regarding rights and duties, that is, is not satisfied with the "normativity" of natural law, which constitutes a specific type of value judgment on the facts, but rather a starting point for "analysis" of all dimensions and aspects of life. To know what is natural just in

[118] Joseph A. Schumpeter, *History of Economic Analysis* (Supreme Council for Culture, 2005), 1:561.

[119] Ibid., 168.

any particular case, it is necessary to analyze the circumstances and generalizations that can be drawn, and it can be called natural law in the analytical sense. Thus, rational philosophy was introduced in connection with natural law, where the "natural reason" constituted the source of the facts that precede experience. Indeed, the natural mind is capable of drawing conclusions about spiritual and existential objects and inferring, for example, about the existence of God.[120]

Physiocrats (i.e., precisely those who assert the supremacy of the role of nature; economists as a cohesive group with a common position), referring to the most prominent of them, François Quinet (1664–1774), Robert-Jacques Turgot (1727–1781), and Pierre-Samuel Debon de Nemours (1739–1817). Their primary and pivotal commitment revolved around the concept of natural law, which they fundamentally regarded as the law governing economic and social behavior.

As for the law of kings and legislators, it can only be accepted to the extent that it aligns with natural law or adds limited value to it. The existence and protection of property rights should be in harmony with natural law, as well as with the freedom of buying and selling, and the necessary steps to ensure the defense of this domain. Wisdom requires allowing matters to proceed according to natural motives and constraints without interference. Moreover, the principle underlying legislation and governance, in general, should be "Let him work, let him pass."[121]

With classical economic thought, the counter-opinion emerges that the modes of production that preceded capitalism did not know the phenomena that economic thought arose to try to explain, market, or criticize. Economic ideas are always and essentially a product of their time and place, and they cannot be viewed separately from the world they explain. As the world changes, these ideas must also change if they are to maintain their importance. Some believe that economics, as a vision of the world, did not develop in its known sense in our current era except with the emergence of capitalism.

---

[120] Ibid., 173.

[121] John Kenneth Galbraith, *History of Economic Thought* (National Council for Culture, Arts, and Literature, 2000), 64.

Despite all the economic data, phenomena, and ideas that preceded it historically, from ancient Greek thought to feudal eras, some see mercantilism not as an economic intellectual system but primarily as a product of the minds of statesmen, senior officials, financiers, and businessmen at the time.[122]

Economic thought developed with Adam Smith, David Ricardo, Karl Marx, Robert Malthus, and others in the eighteenth century. Therefore, the beginnings of liberal capitalist thought begin with these figures from the eighteenth century and continue with all their developments, contexts, and variations up to our present era, including the emergence of neoliberalism. In light of this, our presentation of liberal economic doctrine addresses the ideas circulated within the contexts of thinkers and economic schools of thought within this economic ideological school. We return here to continue our presentation of one of the key pillars in liberal thought within the framework of ideology—namely, natural law and its impact on classical liberal capitalist economic thought, with references to contemporary philosophers who have had a significant influence on shaping economic thought.

Although the primary influential source in classical liberal economic thought is Scholastic thought with its theological dimension, the writings of the natural and divine philosophers have had a significant impact as well. They acknowledge the existence of God but without revelation, and their influence and reference manifest in nature with its laws of wisdom.

[You can refer back to the first part of this work.]

[You can also refer back to the philosophers of natural law: Hobbes, Locke, Descartes, Spinoza, etc.]

Natural law received criticism only from secular historians who viewed it as a mystical and speculative concept.

The continuation of the concept of natural law among the classical capitalist writers, starting from Adam Smith and Marshall to the new liberals (neoliberals), revolved around "it is the law that is superior to any positive law," as Montesquieu put it. And thus it was the

[122] Ibid., 45.

source of many of the theoretical premises that emerged from it (individualism, benefit, economic neutrality of the state, freedom of trade, etc.), as will be mentioned later in the contexts of this book and when examining them. Life for the classical capitalists is organized naturally, and no one should interfere in it, so Smith's economic motives focus on the role of self-interest, and striving for it individually and competitively is the source of the greatest amount of public good. He said this: "We do not expect our food from the benevolence of the butcher, the brewer, or the baker, but rather we expect it from their care for their interests. We are not addressing their humanity, but rather their love for themselves." And he adds after that "in this case, as in many other cases, an invisible hand led him toward achieving an end that was not part of his purpose… And I have never known that much good was achieved at the hands of those who seek the common good. That is a practice that is not common among merchants. To dissuade them, all it takes is the use of very few words."[123]

Similarly, the concepts of utilitarianism and private and public interest among classical capitalist writers were derived from natural law.

One of the prominent figures in this framework is Herbert Spencer (1820–1903), who believed in Darwin's theory of "survival of the fittest." He stated, "Millionaires are the product of natural selection… They are the agents of society selected by the operation of the natural laws to do the work."[124] He argued that they receive high wages and live in luxury, which is beneficial for society. Additionally, in another context, he stated, "Charity also tends to perpetuate the unfit."[125]

This embracement of natural law finds resonance in the shift represented by Neoclassicism, even further bolstering its inception when investigating pure capitalism. Neoclassical economists extol economic liberalism and advocate for the philosophy of natural law as a fundamental source[126] and a starting point for economic analysis.

[123] John Kenneth Galbraith, *History of Economic Thought*, 77.

[124] Ibid., 136.

[125] Ibid., 137.

[126] Wisam al-Malak, Evolution of Economic Thought (Al-Minhal Al-Lubnani Publishing House, 2012), part 2, 7.

The ideas of Herbert Spencer found a complete expression about a century later in the works of the neoclassical economist Milton Friedman.[127]

The situational philosophy. It is evident that the formation of scientific doctrine is based on a philosophical perspective, and economics, which began to take its scope in the known form in our current era, since the eighteenth century (starting with Adam Smith, Ricardo, Malthus, etc.), was based in its philosophical background on philosophical insights. It has extensions and sources that preceded its existence and settled with the liberal doctrine within the framework of positivist philosophy, which finds its roots in the Greek empirical philosophical doctrine conceived by Aristotle, the Epicureans, and the Sophists and developed by English thinkers in the seventeenth and eighteenth centuries (Hobbes, Locke, Hume). This experimental, or sensory, doctrine assumes that all human knowledge is derived from experience, which reflects the sensory impressions received by the human mind, since the mind before this experience is devoid of any purposeful activity of its own, and that impressions are the final elements into which all mental phenomena can be transformed.

The developments in the field of natural sciences based on experiments, especially physics, and their coincidence with that historical period tempted some liberal thinkers to extend the experimental method to the social sciences, including economics. Thus, any scientific knowledge must gain its credibility through empirical testing, negating any metaphysical or occult knowledge.

Auguste Comte (1798–1857), who sought to adopt the methods of the natural sciences based on generalization from historical facts, focused on social evolution or, as he termed it, "the law of three stages." According to his philosophy, human thought evolves through three stages:

a) *The theological stage.* This is where human thinking begins under the influence of imagination (mythol-

[127] John Kenneth Galbraith, *History of Economic Thought*, 137.

ogy) and explains phenomena by attributing them to supernatural causes.

b) *The metaphysical stage.* This stage involves seeking causes for phenomena and attaining knowledge through an abstract external force capable on its own of causing all observed phenomena. It assumes the existence of the mind to explain psychological phenomena.

c) *The scientific stage.* This stage represents the maturity of the mind, where life is subjected to reality and experiments. Here, relative knowledge, not absolute, becomes apparent, and metaphysical abstractions are rejected. This stage is considered the decisive phase in the stages of human thought.

The influence of this philosophy on economic analysis includes interpreting phenomena and events based on their causes and outcomes, assessing moral judgments, examining the effects of variable causal factors on functional variables, and deriving theories within the framework of specific relative phenomena. However, this does not constitute an intellectual method for forming an abstract overall perspective. Consequently, scientific facts in the social realm are confined to sensory perceptions capable of discovering laws governing social issues.

The most significant development of this philosophy in influencing economic analysis came from Austrian thinkers and philosophers in the twentieth century through what they termed "logical positivism." This movement began with Moritz Schlick (1882–1936) and Rudolf Carnap (1891–1970), among others from the Austrian school. They believed that scientific knowledge is acquired solely through sensory experience, and logical analysis is the only method to obtain this knowledge.

Accordingly, all issues that involve religious, philosophical, and moral concepts are empty and meaningless, or they are merely descriptions of internal feelings and sensations. The necessary and sufficient condition for a judgment to take a rational and scientific form is that it be capable of being tested by practical experience and sensory observation.[128]

Rationale. The capitalist classicists in their search for the correct behavior in man. They were guided, through natural laws, to rationality in man, and it is evident in Cartesian rational thought in his book *Meditations on First Philosophy.* Descartes (1596–1650) did not confine thought to rationality, will, and imagination. He also addressed sensation. According to Descartes, human perfection lies in rational decision-making and sound judgment. This perspective was adopted by classical capitalist thought, despite Descartes being considered a metaphysical philosopher who believed in the existence of God but rejected faith in revelation and prophets (divine). He did not accept the idea of God's intervention in clarifying thought, adhering to his rational inclination. Descartes used thought in a broad sense that is almost synonymous with the process of awareness.[129]

Freedom. Derived from natural law, it is closely linked to rational human beings, guiding their human behavior. This topic was discussed in the first part of this book under the chapter "Freedom of Will," and it can be referred to there to avoid repetition. Here, we simply note its reflection in economics within the practical scope: "Let producers work freely, and if they fail, they will bear the consequences of their failure and leave the market arena. This is how people work, think, produce, and contract."[130]

This freedom extends into the practical realm, and it is what obscured the name of the liberal (free) doctrine and took its scope into the economic field (the free economic system, freedom of trade, freedom of ownership, etc.), and it also formed for economic analysis its basic value perspective, whether in formulating theory or deter-

[128] Hassan Agha Nazari, *Theorizing in Islamic Economics* (Civilization Center for the Development of Islamic Thought, 2012), 34–35.

[129] Mohamed Kazem Al Mouhajir, *Theses in Comparative Economic Thought between the West and Islam* (Dar Al-Balaghah, 2015), 22.

[130] Adam Smith from Mustafa Sheha, *Economics* (University Publishing House, 1986), 441.

mining the causality of the movement of factors affecting economic phenomena, the independent variables, and the indicative variable.

Individualism and utilitarianism. Personal interest and public interest are very ancient principles, garnering wide intellectual attention in most ancient civilizations. They shaped Greek thought as well as Scholastic thought as important sources for classical economists. Around the mid-eighteenth century, they manifested strongly in the field of social and economic thought as the philosophy of life (i.e., the idea of the basic forces that drive life and economic efforts), through which many economic data are determined in interpreting phenomena and drawing economic policies. For classical economists, the basic premise stems from the fundamental driver of humanity—namely, the individual's pursuit of happiness and obtaining goods that satisfy their desires. This pursuit can be facilitated in the best way if obstacles are removed from its path, primarily governmental or social obstacles. Thus, within the context of natural law, individualism becomes a central and normative axis that defines fundamental positions in the course of life. This includes the stance on the economic role of the state (which we will discuss in the subsequent section under the title of Mechanism) as well as issues such as individual rights and public rights (justice), among others, which will be addressed in this work.

All contexts of analysis by classical economists and even contemporary liberals deal with individualism as a natural premise, upon which every explanatory perspective or policy framework in economics is built. With Adam Smith, we see that anyone working for personal gain is simultaneously working for the benefit of society, based on the premise that social interest is nothing but the sum of individuals' interests. In this way, individual interest is linked to the incentive that drives individuals to pursue their interests. This explains the efficiency and progress of the capitalist system through individual motives and incentives, according to their claims. Thus, in this context, the interest of society is nothing but a quantitative sum of the interests of individuals.

The French poet and philosopher Voltaire (1694–1778) celebrated individuality in his struggle against religious authorities, as seen in his famous essay "Crush the Infamy."[131]

The principle of individualism takes on an extreme and sharp meaning for some liberal thinkers. For instance, Helvetius (1715–1771) considered the principle of personal interest in the social world to be analogous to the law of gravity in the natural world, while Beccaria (1764) went so far as to the point of stressing that humans are entirely selfish and individualistic, caring nothing for the interests of others.[132] Meanwhile, Hobbes viewed humans as wolves to their fellow humans, existing in a state characterized by aggression, fear, malice, and seeking harm to others, with life centered on the pursuit of their desires.

Individualism takes a fundamental dimension in the thought and methodologies of the new liberals who see that the preferred method for studying economic phenomena lies in looking from the perspective of the individual as both the determinant and actor. They argue that society has nothing essential beyond the actions of individuals. The liberal economist Ludwig von Mises (1881–1973) offers criticism of what he calls the "holistic concept," which starts from the whole rather than from the individual who constitutes the element from which the whole takes shape. Based on this approach, he launched his attack on socialism and central planning.

Individualism, as discussed above, is closely linked to utility, which finds its roots initially among the Epicureans under the exploration of pleasure and pain in humans. This concept was further developed by English economists in the eighteenth century and progressed in the nineteenth century. From the perspective we mentioned earlier, as a driving force for economic efforts and life through the individual's pursuit of happiness (replacing pleasure from the Epicureans with happiness among utilitarian economists), the principle of the common interest was formulated. This principle suggests that the pleasures and pains of each individual are quanti-

[131] Will Durant, *The Story of Philosophy* (Al-Maaref Library, 1985), 492.
[132] Joseph A. Schumpeter, *History of Economic Analysis*, part 1, 196–197.

fiable quantities that can be forcibly added to a quantity known as individual happiness. This individual happiness is then reassembled into a social aggregate, which corresponds to the public interest or societal well-being. From this arose the utilitarian doctrine advocating for maximizing happiness for the greatest number of individuals, thus reducing the global world of human values to a utilitarian scheme resembling a law. The credit for shaping this doctrine goes to Jeremy Bentham (1748–1832) and John Stuart Mill, whose work *Three Essays on Religion* was published posthumously in 1874.[133]

The new liberals, or neoliberals, in their renewal of classical capitalist thought, without abandoning their position within Adam Smith's world, manifested their ideas around utility in the form of "marginal utility." This concept emerged in the writings of Jevons, Menger, and Walras in the latter half of the nineteenth century. They based their concepts of marginal utility and its utilization to the fullest extent in economic analysis on the famous laws of the German economist Gossen in his work *Laws of Human Relations* (1854):

a) *The law of prolongation.* This means that when every pleasure continues without interruption, its intensity, after being initially high, decreases until it eventually becomes nonexistent.
b) *The law of repetition.* When the feeling of pleasure is repeated, the degree of intensity and duration of pleasure decreases with each repetition, so intensity and duration decrease more rapidly if the repetitions are repeated more quickly.[134]

Through these laws, the marginal law emerged: "An individual pushes his utility to its maximum level when he allocates his money to acquire a combination of goods in such a way that the satisfaction obtained from the last monetary unit spent on each good is equal."[135]

---

133 Ibid., 2:50.

134 Wisam al-Malak, *Evolution of Economic Thought*, part 2, 61–62.

135 Ibid., 36.

2. The purpose.

It is very clear through classical capitalist thought that the ultimate aim of economic activity is profit in harmony with the individualism, utility, and rationality characteristic of this ideology. It aims to maximize utility for the individual, whether as a producer or consumer, and becomes a general assumption in this thought. Economists like Senor consider it one of its fundamental assumptions,[136] if not the first assumption ("each individual seeks to obtain additional wealth with the least possible sacrifice"), and considers it the basis of theoretical thinking. In the same context, this aligns with the texts of Ricardo and Malthus, as well as with Adam Smith and John Stuart Mill, where each individual seeks to maximize the difference between their total satisfaction and total sacrifices, with both being discounted according to the current moment.[137]

Therefore, the primary objective of the capitalist production line is profit, and this is coupled with the presence of the perfect competitive situation imposed by the capitalist mode of production, which sets the conditions for perfect competition as a necessary condition that constitutes the motivation for development and progress, as the determinants of this impose:

a) The presence of several producers, and no one of them alone can influence the quantity of product supply or prices.
b) Denying the presence of obstacles to the entry of new investors, while being able to obtain sufficient capital to finance their projects.
c) Any increase in production resulting from the entry of new investors will not affect prices.
d) The ability to obtain the elements of production without anyone controlling it through monopoly. The exit

[136] Senor's four assumptions can be found in Joseph A. Schumpeter, *History of Economic Analysis*, 2:276–293.

[137] Schumpeter, *History of Economic Analysis*, 2:276–277.

> of producers from the market will not have an impact on supply or prices.

This tendency or perspective on the issue of competition, with the rise of marginal thinking or the marginalist school in production and the discussion of diminishing returns due to expansion (the theory of diminishing returns), will adopt another tendency. There will be a shift toward a greater focus on seeking to maximize profits through monopolization. The economists Marshall and Pigou paved the way for this, asserting that a firm with increasing returns has an interest in expanding its size to become monopolistic. This allows it to reduce its marginal and average costs. Therefore, they consider that increasing the size of the firm is a crucial positive aspect.[138]

At the beginning of the twentieth century, there was a call for the necessity of abandoning perfect competition and adopting another tendency based on monopolization, paving the way for what is known as the revolution of imperfect competition, or what the American economist Chamberlain (1899–1967) called the theory of monopolistic competition. Similarly, the economist Robinson played the same role in Britain in the thirties of the last century with the same formulation.

This tendency to blend competition and monopolization is based on a foundation of realistic analysis. Competition doesn't just occur through prices but also choices in production methods, product selection, sales policies, and production inputs. Competition may be imperfect due to the limited number of firms, their size, and their degree of concentration. In reality, actual competition exists between firms with different sizes, costs, perspectives, and policies. They strive to develop production methods and introduce escalating variations in the quality and models of products as well as the development of new products.[139]

This analytical tendency justifies the existence of international monopolistic cartels, including those with multinational character-

[138] Wisam al-Malak, *Evolution of Economic Thought*, part 2, 411.

[139] Wisam al-Malak, *Evolution of Economic Thought*, part 2, 415–416.

istics. Despite this analysis coming from modernists and coinciding with the new liberals, it has not been immune from the voices of some new liberals advocating for a return to a purer form of capitalism. Among them, we witness the attack by Professor Friedrich Hayek staunchly defending the principles of classical economics: "The price system will not fulfill its role unless competition prevails, meaning when the individual producer becomes bound to adapt to changes in prices and is unable to control them."[140]

3. The tool.

The tool through which the capitalist economic system operates is very clear across the contexts of starting points and formation based on individualism, utilitarianism, and absolute commercial freedom, which is "private property." Its existence aligns with natural law and consequently aligns with both domestic and international trade freedom, allowing matters to proceed according to natural incentives and constraints without interference. Economic motives are inherently competitive, serving as the primary source of the greatest public good, with the public interest merely being the aggregation of individual interests. Despite being ancient, these principles manifested strongly among classical economists from the mid-eighteenth century, starting with Adam Smith and Ricardo, the proponent of the "invisible hand" concept, who emphasizes that goodness stems from this aspect of private property, refuting the notion that the public interest is the source of goodness.[141]

Furthermore, advocates of the utilitarian doctrine, starting from Bentham, emphasize that the primary driving force of humanity is the individual's pursuit of happiness and obtaining goods that serve this purpose. This pursuit manifests in its best form when obstacles—whether governmental or social interventions, controls, and organi-

---

[140] Friedrich A. von Hayek, *The Road to Serfdom* (Chicago University Publishing Department, 1944), 49, From Kenneth Galbraith, *History of Economic Thought*, 267.

[141] Galbraith, *History of Economic Thought*, 77.

zations[142]—are minimized. Indeed, the writer Beccaria (1764) went as far as to emphasize that humans are entirely selfish and individualistic, caring little for the interests of others or the public good.[143]

Accordingly, the contexts of the public sector and its connection to the state were confined to a narrow scope defined by the tasks of the state, denying the economic role of the state except in certain specific circumstances, especially during economic crises. Capitalist economists would differ from these starting points by calling for state intervention, especially the economic thinker Keynes. We will return to discussing this topic in the following section when we talk about the performance mechanism of the capitalist system.

As for our contemporary history, and within the context of neoliberals,_____.

And their call for a return to a purer capitalism. Their desired positions are evident in the call to prevent everything that hinders the freedom of the private sector's performance and to eliminate any role for the public sector. Indeed, denying its existence and limiting the state's economic role to protecting the private sector. Any other role for the state will create poverty as the contemporary economic writer Gilder claimed.[144]

4. Performance mechanism.

The performance mechanism in classical liberal thought is closely tied to the theoretical principles we mentioned earlier—namely, individualism, utilitarianism, freedom, natural law, and rationality. In the absence of a significant economic role for the state (which we will discuss later), the mechanism operates through market economics and the automatic performance of the capitalist system. The market is the meeting point of producers as sellers and consumers as buyers. Prices within the market determine the behavior of producers in supply and also influence the behavior of consumers

---

[142] Ibid., 132.

[143] Ibid., 196–197.

[144] Wisam al-Malak, *Evolution of Economic Thought*, part 2, 711–714.

in demand. Through this process, market mechanisms unfold by the intellectual principles of capitalism as follows.

The fundamental issue that poses a dilemma in satisfaction, whether for producers or consumers, lies in scarcity and utility. Scarcity arises from the balance between increasing needs and limited resources while utility refers to the maximization of benefits for producers or consumers. While capitalist economics acknowledges that utility is based on a psychological foundation related to individual desire, it assumes the transformation of this desire into action (purchasing power for consumers and capital power for producers), and it operates based on wealth distribution. For a producer to be able to produce goods that satisfy consumers' desires and offer them the utility they seek, while also maximizing profit and minimizing costs, they must engage in appropriate economic calculations. They receive indicators through market mechanisms and price systems, where the convergence occurs between consumer desires and producer responses to meet those desires. Therefore, the market is a center of convergence and agreement between supply and demand forces, where the final result in resource allocation occurs naturally and automatically, without any intervention from a central authority. Hence, classical capitalist thought posits that the capitalist system is a natural system that operates according to instinct, without any intervention, surpassing individual wills. It organizes production, distribution, and circulation of production through the price system and market.[145]

One of the basic pillars of this intellectual framework above is based on the principle of nonintervention by any central authority (the state) in the context of the functioning of this system. This emphasis is evident through the intensive propositions of classical liberal economists, who argue that the primary driving force of humanity is the individual's pursuit of happiness and obtaining goods that serve that end. Second, they assert that this pursuit progresses optimally with

[145] Mohamed Kazem Al Mouhajir, *Theses in Comparative Economic Thought between the West and Islam*, 27–29.

minimal governmental or other social obstacles, whether in the form of guidance, intervention, prohibition, control, or organization.[146]

Consequently, the classical economists believed, as J. S. Mill formulated it, that the policy of noninterference represented the general rule for a country and that what was expressively called "government intervention" was the exception.[147] In the general context, Gilder asserts that "the protecting state is the one that creates poverty while claiming to limit it."[148]

This general principle is often found in some liberal economic thinkers with a corresponding approach to it on the issue of the state's economic role, especially during economic crises of the capitalist system and recession cycles. The most prominent stance in this context comes from the prominent contemporary economist John Maynard Keynes (1883–1946), as well as contemporary economists such as William Trufant Foster (1879–1950) and Waddill Catchings (1879–1967), who launched intensive campaigns urging the government to intervene forcefully to support and enhance demand, attacking the Say's law and the economic beliefs based on it. In the face of the global economic crisis of 1929, the basics advocated by Keynes were simple and clearly articulated to launch an anti-depression policy away from its classical shackles. Keynes argued that the modern economy does not necessarily find its equilibrium in full employment, but it can find this equilibrium in the presence of unemployment (what he called "underemployment equilibrium") and that "Say's law" was no longer valid. There could be a deficiency in demand, so the government can and should take steps to overcome this situation. Thus, the underemployment equilibrium and the abandonment of "Say's law" and the government's call for deficit spending to support demand are the essence of the Keynesian system, and from now on, the state will be responsible for the overall performance of the economy.[149]

Once again, with intensified inclinations toward contemporary neoliberalism, especially advocated by Hayek, Friedman, and Gilder,

[146] John Kenneth Galbraith, *History of Economic Thought*, 132.
[147] Joseph A. Schumpeter, *History of Economic Analysis*, 239.
[148] Wisam al-Malak, *Evolution of Economic Thought*, 712.
[149] John Kenneth Galbraith, *History of Economic Thought*, 239–254.

calling for a return to pure capitalism far from any interference of the state in the economy, they advocate a return to interpreting economic behavior through neoclassical theory regarding prices. They insist on the state refraining from any intervention leading to tangible alterations in resource allocation, thereby undermining Keynesian theories.

Moreover, once again, and within the context of the global economic crisis (2008–2009), the call for the state's economic role returned strongly, and French president Nicolas Sarkozy declared, "Noninterference has ended, and with it, the all-powerful, most knowledgeable market has ended."[150]

The fundamental principle of capitalism, particularly within the framework of the market mechanism, relies prominently on perfect competition. It is a cornerstone in all contexts of classical liberal thought. However, this principle is often violated in the face of the economic realities and the prevailing conditions in global markets, where companies strive to maximize profit.

Marshall and Pigou affirm that an enterprise with increasing returns has an interest in growing in size until it becomes monopolistic. It allows the enterprise to reduce its fixed and average costs. Consequently, this analysis leads to the consideration that the expansion in the size of the enterprise is a crucial positive as concentration becomes an inevitable law within an economy witnessing escalating returns and economies of scale.[151]

This approach was further developed by P. Sraffa, who analyzed monopolies and argued for the abandonment of perfect competition in favor of a different approach centered on monopoly. It laid the groundwork for what came to be known as the "imperfect competition revolution," which emerged in the United States and Britain through the work of American economist Edward Chamberlin (1899–1967) and British economist Joan Robinson from 1927 to 1933. This revolution introduced a new theory that integrated

---

150 Paul Mason, *The Coming Global Crisis* (Printing Company for publishing and distribution, 2012), 85.

151 Wisam al-Malak, *Evolution of Economic Thought*, 411.

elements of both competition and monopoly. Published in 1933, this theory challenged the notion that perfect competition could be applied to real-world economic systems. Instead, it proposed the concept of "monopolistic competition," where competition and monopoly coexist within the same system. This approach acknowledged the presence of large corporations and cartels, effectively legislating for monopolies alongside competition.

We have presented an overview of the liberal economic doctrine, outlining its basic principles and foundations, without claiming comprehensiveness or exhaustive coverage from all perspectives. Achieving such in depth would require a more extensive and detailed study. However, what we have presented, in our view, serves a purpose within the context of our discussion. Our critical opinions on this presentation and our intellectual observations can be addressed within our attempt to outline the Islamic economic doctrine, which we will discuss in the following section.

Chapter 9

The Islamic Economic Doctrine: Foundational Perspective

Islam is not just a religion that clarifies the relationship between the Creator and the created but rather a religion that addresses the philosophy of existence and sources of knowledge. It establishes rules and legislations for life and sets moral standards for human behavior and the interpretation of phenomena. Within its overall framework and in the contexts of economic life, it carries in its message the contexts of life, potentials, data, and rulings from which an economic doctrine emerges by its determinants in beliefs, standards, perspectives, and their reflections in the contexts of practical worldly life. Therefore, understanding it within its doctrinal framework is the scope of our discussion in this excerpt as an initial project and intellectual effort for prospects that accumulate and evolve with the emergence of Islamic thinkers, succeeding one another, to take their intellectual endeavor to an advanced level of economic knowledge and to establish broader contexts for human happiness.

The contexts shaping the development of liberal capitalist economic thought, as we have presented above and according to historical stages that spanned centuries and continue to unfold, are rationalized by economists like Kenneth Galbraith and others as being products of their time and place. They argue that economic ideas are fundamentally shaped by the world they interpret, and as the world changes continuously, these ideas must also change to remain relevant.[152] This perspective is linked to a theoretical background concerning the issue of existence and creation as well as to a theory of knowledge that restricts its sources through sensory pathways, as we discussed in the first part of this work. It is also linked to existential realities and their developmental trajectory according to the sociopolitical structure that is in a continuous state of flux, particularly in Europe. Therefore, the trajectory of liberal economic doctrine, as we have outlined, is nothing but a reflection of the thought and realities of Western society in a specific period, its presence remaining until our contemporary era.

In a context that's different in its formative approach to what was mentioned above, Islamic thought emerges based on its perspective in the philosophy of existence, as well as the theory of knowledge, as a created reality, as we presented in the first part of this book. Accordingly, it is associated with the given divine revelation at its foundation as divine enlightenment. It also coincides with rational proof in a complementary crucible as achieving certainty cannot be achieved unless it is illuminated by the light of Sharia and supported by reason, according to the Islamic perspective.

Whereas economic thought as a case is investigated within a specific framework under this title, it is not explicitly spoken in Islamic thought, but its seeds exist within a comprehensive framework that addresses the aspects of human existence and life in both its worldly dimensions and the afterlife as well as its spiritual and materialistic aspects and its social, economic, political, cultural, educational and behavioral effects, and so on. Through these seeds, the Islamic message is directed to the individual, society, and state, wherever they exist in this universe, and not exclusively in specific Islamic systems. From this standpoint, and within the actual tasks assigned to it, and by the requirements of the stages of development and the necessities of life that surround this world, we must have a rational deductive context that establishes an economic doctrine. Islamic in contemporary dimensions through the contexts of Islamic thought. Of course, such work requires intellectual efforts that may take the

[152] John Kenneth Galbraith, *History of Economic Thought*, 16.

context of research teams of Islamic thinkers whose intellectual knowledge extends along with intellectual ability in the economic field to intellectual ability in Islamic thought and Sharia. My efforts in this context and this book are an incentive to stimulate thought in this field, one that can develop the foundation for the Islamic economic doctrine that I will discuss in this work, taking into account all the standards and methods of research methodologies and guidance described by previous Islamic thinkers.

I reaffirm the tendency of crystallizing the Islamic economic doctrine, in its rulings—which are characterized by totality and absoluteness in terms of time and place—and their orientation toward humanity, individuals, communities, and nations alike. They are also characterized by the normative nature of what should be, not what is, and constitute a specific perspective as theoretical wisdom that directs the tendency of practical wisdom in interpreting and treating phenomena in societies in their contemporary evolutionary forms and by the axes that we have referred to as a systematic scientific framework (ideology, finalism, tool, performance mechanism).

Accordingly, we present the foundational perspective of the Islamic economic doctrine according to the contexts that will follow.

It remains essential to point out an important methodological issue in formulating the foundation of an Islamic economic doctrine. The integration of Islamic thought, based on revelation and reason and Sharia through its sources as a religion characterized by comprehensiveness and integration, has given a functional role to reason in keeping pace with the developments in social, economic, and technological realms and the like. Therefore, asserting the comprehensiveness of religion in its rulings and across historical evolutionary stages without considering the role of reason in analyzing emerging data and issuing specific judgments undermines the doctrinal principle of the role of reason. There is room for the convergence of reason and revelation and for reinforcing reason with Sharia. The economic doctrine comprises ideological and normative judgments characterized by comprehensiveness and universality, where practical contexts are included in the fields of economic analysis. They establish the correct context for the convergence of general judgments with relative, partial, and specific judgments. That is, moving from the general to the specific and aligning evolving societal data with Sharia rulings. We find that the Islamic economic doctrine is limited in its basic lines and axes to general formulations whose practical dimensions are adapted to contemporary circumstances through economic analysis, which we will address in the third part of this book.

9.1 Ideology

Before delving into the fundamental pillars of Islamic economic thought as a doctrine, it is necessary to briefly refer to the philosophical background regarding reason. Although we extensively discussed this philosophical background in the first part, from the economic perspective, reaffirming the trajectory of Islamic thought may be redundant. However, it is indispensable. Islamic thought believes in divine reality, which posits an external reality to the world and nature, attributing both matter and spirit to a deeper cause beyond them. This divine concept of the world never implies dispensing with natural causes or rebelling against any facts of the world. Instead, it is a concept that considers Allah as the deeper cause, necessitating that the sequence of causes and effects ascend to a force beyond nature and matter. Thus, any contradiction between it and any scientific fact disappears completely because it allows for the widest exploration of the secrets of nature and its system while retaining divine interpretation, ultimately placing the deep cause in a principle higher than nature and matter.[153] In the context of the mechanism of knowledge through the methodology of rational doctrine, it elucidates that human knowledge is divided into two types: necessary (or intuitive) knowledge, to which the soul must submit without demanding proof or evidence of its correctness, and theoretical knowledge and information that the soul does not believe in its correctness except in the light of previous knowledge and information. The judgment on them depends on the process of thinking and inference.

---

[153] Muhammad Baqir al-Sadr, *Our Philosophy* (Al Taarof Publishing House, 1982), 180.

Accordingly, the first criterion for human thinking, in general, is the necessary actual knowledge as it is the indispensable foundation in every field, and the truth and error of every idea must be measured considering it. Thus, the field of human knowledge becomes broader than the limits of sense and experience because it equips human thought with energies that deal with facts and issues beyond matter. This does not mean that rationalist doctrine transcends the role of experience in human science and knowledge and the huge services it has provided to humanity, whether in secrets of the universe or the mysteries of nature that it has revealed. It can never be overcome, but it is believed that experience alone could not have played this tremendous role because deducing any scientific fact requires the application of the necessary actual laws, meaning that this conclusion is made in the light of primary knowledge, and the experiment itself cannot be the fundamental and primary source of knowledge.[154]

Based on this philosophical approach grounded in divine realism and according to the rational doctrine embraced by Islam with an infinite spirit capable of everything, knowledgeable of everything, He created the universe according to a divine cosmic system, addressing existence and evolution and known through revelation and messengers.

"Indeed, We sent Our messengers with clear proofs, and We revealed with them the Scripture and the balance that people may maintain [their affairs] in justice."[155]

This religious doctrinal given is completely consistent with the philosophical given based on the mind as the mind is a law from within, and the law is a mind from the outside. In the words of Abu Hamid Al-Ghazali, "The mind is indispensable to hearing, and hearing is indispensable to the mind. The one who calls for pure imitation while isolating the mind is ignorant, and the one who is satisfied with mere action without the lights of transmission is arrogant. So

---

[154] Muhammad Baqir al-Sadr, *Our Philosophy*, 63–64.

[155] Surah al-Hadid, verse 25.

beware of being from one of the two groups, and be one who combines the two principles."[156]

Through this perspective, the sources of Islamic thought are defined, containing ideas, insights, indicators, principles, and economic laws that require scientific efforts and enlightened thinking capable of placing them in contemporary scientific contexts and frameworks, thus becoming part of the message of knowledge over the foreseeable time horizon. The sources within the framework of transmission in Islamic thought are based on the Quran and the noble prophetic tradition, and within the framework of reason, they are based on rulings derived from Islamic law through scholarly endeavor as well as the sayings of the Imams and scholars proficient in interpretation, who are capable of ijtihad. Based on our reference to transmitted traditions and reason, and within the economic framework we are addressing, the foundations and principles of Islamic thought emerge as a doctrinal framework indicating its context encompassing the general, standard, and relative aspects within its practical framework, as outlined below.

9.1.1 Human centrality and self-perfection

Indeed, Allah has placed humanity as the center of the universe and existence, where meanings and actions meet. He described human beings with a characteristic of perfection: "Verily, we created man in the best stature."[157] And this is in terms of creation, as a creature, but in pursuit of perfection, He described humanity according to His will within a framework and a path defined by knowledge and faith: "Allah will raise in degrees those of you who have believed and those who were given knowledge by degrees."[158] Believing and having faith in the divine message conveyed by the prophets through revela-

---

[156] Abu Hamid al-Ghazali: *Revival of the Religious Sciences* (Al-Halabi Library and Printing Press, 1939), 16.
Hadi Fadlallah, *Introduction to Philosophy* (Al-Mawasem Publishing House, 2004), 63.

[157] Surah Al-Tin, verse 4.

[158] Surah Al-Moujadala, verse 11.

tion and adhering to the approach in worldly conduct according to the dictates of the divine law. As for knowledge, it is the comprehensive organized understanding that provides a general perception of the universe and life. In other words, the sources of knowledge and human perfection are based on divine law and reason. Knowledge holds a lofty meaning in human perfection as it is an attribute of God. God is the All-Knowing as an attribute of the divine essence, and it has been bestowed upon human beings to bring them closer to perfection. The difference between the two lies in the distinction between the constant and the variable.[159]

Within the context of the relationship between reason and religious law (Sharia), some may have questions that need clarification. First, regarding human behavior within the framework of religious law supporting reason, it may be perceived as restricting human freedom, which is inherent. Consequently, this might suggest a denial of human perfection. We have extensively addressed this question in the first part of this book under the concept of freedom. I don't see the need to repeat it here, but I refer the reader back to the discussion on freedom in the first part of the book, where a comprehensive answer to this question is provided.

The other question within this context is formulated as follows:

> As long as Islamic law (Sharia) encompasses all aspects of life, including its economic dimensions, and is characterized by stability in its essential aspects, while human societies are witnessing evolution and transformation in relationships, modes of living, human interaction with nature, and even interpersonal relations between consumers and producers or among individuals, especially in our contemporary setting which has experienced profound and comprehensive cognitive and scientific development, how can reason

[159] Hassan Hanafi, *Concepts Of Science—Work and Social Solidarity in Arab Islamic Thought* (United Nations, 1988), 7.

> keep pace with this progress and provide contemporary judgments that align with the realities of this era without conflicting with Sharia?

Our answer to this question must be based on the following principles.

In the divine cosmic order that places humans at the center and supports reason with Sharia, the functional role of reason based on knowledge and understanding must be consistent and integrated with Sharia. Any denial of the role of reason through the comprehensiveness and stability of Sharia implies a denial of any progression in human perfection toward the Creator. It also signifies a stagnation where reason cannot keep up with societal developments and cannot issue judgments for evolving or novel situations. Therefore, the concept of ijtihad as an inductive issue has contemporary implications, giving reason to its existential role in the divine cosmic order.

In the rulings of Sharia, there are judgments characterized by their universality and generality regarding time and place. These are fixed rulings that cannot be changed, which we can describe as the "solid core" of Sharia. However, within their universality, they contain principles that can accommodate evolving situations and align with the objectives of Sharia. For example, in economic matters, Sharia mandates "fulfilling contracts"[160] and prohibits transactions involving haram (forbidden) elements like *riba* (usury). Through the role of the reason in adapting this starting point according to the newly presented situation, it can issue rulings that are compatible with the purposes of the Sharia through deduction and rooting the ruling based on the Sharia starting point in its overall form so that the title of the situation in its partial or relative form falls under it.

In Sharia rulings, which are based on specific temporal and spatial considerations, or rulings that can be subject to evolutionary and innovative factors, dealing with them using contemporary rational judgments must always be based in harmony with Sharia. This is a fundamental principle in issuing contemporary judgments,

---

[160] Surah Al-Maida, verse 1.

and it must be rooted in derivation from recognized Sharia sources. In other cases, judgments may need to be reconsidered considering contemporary societal conditions.

For example, in the context of land ownership, the ruling regarding land ownership for those who invest in and develop it may not align with the technological advancements of today. With modern technology, vast areas of land can be cultivated or enriched in a short period. In such a case, can we permit ownership to those who invest in and develop the land? Of course, this may not be feasible in our contemporary situation. Instead, there may be other solutions, arising from the objectives of Sharia, that can lead to different judgments. We will address this further when discussing the topic of property in the third part of this book, which focuses on economic analysis.

Through these starting points, we will find that the Sharia, with its comprehensive and absolute rulings and its judgments linked to temporal and spatial facts or situations that require ratification, we find that it contains open loops to meet the process of societal development, whether man's relationship with others, society, or his relationship with nature, through our diligent reason that deduces the rulings by the purposes of the Sharia. That is where our opinion is formed, in which we see the comprehensiveness of Sharia law and the arbitration of the role of reason as a complementary state that gives the mind a functional role assigned to it as part of the divine cosmic order. Thus we ensure Sharia's contemporary presence that plays its comprehensive role in all aspects of life.

9.1.2 Individual and society

Human beings are social creatures, regardless of the theories put forth by sociologists regarding the motives and drivers of their social nature. Whether innate, acquired due to the necessities of life, or a natural requirement, the social aspect of humanity is undeniable.

However, in terms of the outcome, it acknowledges the social aspect of humanity. Regarding the relationship between the individual and society, liberal thought, as previously discussed, argues that social welfare is nothing but the sum of individual interests. Therefore, it aligns with its individualistic principles and forms the basis for concepts of justice, freedom, and the like. On the contrary, Marxist thought sees society as absorbing the individual, with their interest merely a reflection of societal interest. Here, the Islamic perspective is presented not only from its historical formation at the outset of these ideas but also in its contemporary presence, rooted in these principles to establish a balanced state between the individual and society.

In the introduction to this book, I wrote about a contemporary human considering the dominance of liberal thought and the era of globalization (a new human like that imposed by liberal economic theory, characterized by illusory maturity, keen on his individual and personal interest, cautious and selfish, unable to comprehend the essence of truth, nobility, or human sublimity). Contemporary liberal thinkers acknowledge this, and in our view, what leads to this lies in the pattern and lifestyle of a human being in a society governed by liberal systems with individualistic rules and utilitarian motives.

The theoretical foundations in Islam revolve around two axes, stemming from its perspective on existence and based on the dimensions of reason (intellect) and revelation:

a) It addresses the individual in his journey toward perfection (as exemplified in the Quranic verse "in the best of stature")[161] to prevent him from descending into lower realms. Islam addresses the conscience of the individual to become upright in behavior and to adhere to religious principles internally. This is achieved through a system of values that dictate specific behavior in life. For example, in the economic realm, there is guidance toward prudence (such as prohibiting extravagance, hoarding, preserving the rights of others, prohibiting cheating and oppression, helping others, relieving the distressed, and so forth). In other words, there is an educational pattern based on vir-

[161] Surah Al-Tin, verse 4.

tue that prevents individuals from succumbing to hedonistic desires and promotes rational self-interest focused on virtue. It inspires human perfection characterized by righteousness, aligning with the community described as "the solid structure."

b) On the other hand, the Islamic perspective does not focus solely on the conscience of the individual but also establishes specific guidelines to prevent human behavior from drifting toward vice. This is done through the rules of Sharia (Islamic law). Examining jurisprudence in the economic field presents us with numerous rulings and principles under the category of "transactions," which define the basis of economic interactions between individuals and groups. Whether in contracts, buying and selling, the ethics of dealings and transactions, or safeguarding the rights of individuals and society, Sharia serves as an external legislator that individuals are obligated to adhere to. When violated, it has consequences such as punishments in this worldly life. It sets standards for the conduct between individuals and society, preventing harm to others and the community (as seen in the principle of "no harm shall be inflicted or reciprocated" and the concept that averting harm takes precedence over securing benefits, especially if the harm is widespread). These rules governing individual and societal behavior do not mean an absolute infringement on human freedom, as discussed in the first part of this book under the section on the concept of free will. Rather, they reinforce it, granting the possibility to create a balanced, integrated society that guides individuals toward perfection.

9.1.3 Motives of human voluntary action

At first glance, the inclusion of this section may seem out of place to the reader. After all, the issue of human volitional motives falls under the realm of practical reasoning or practical wisdom, so how can we categorize it under the title of "ideology" or "theoretical wisdom"? The Islamic perspective on this matter emerges from a theoretical viewpoint in interpreting the volitional behavior of humans. We address this chapter to explain its significance with dimensions that form a spiritual essence for humans, reflecting its influence on the material satisfaction of desires and impulses within them.

We have presented the motives of volitional action in liberal capitalist thought, which stem from the perspective of pleasure and pain, evolving into the concept of happiness. Consequently, utility became the decisive criterion in determining good and evil. However, if the motives of happiness, pleasure, and pain have gained importance among some Islamic thinkers, it does not necessarily mean endorsing this specific Islamic perspective, consistent with liberal thinking. Instead, there is another opposing perspective that can be derived from fundamental intellectual sources, as outlined below.

Islamic thought, in its interpretive positions on phenomena, generally relies on its principles, foundations, and view of existence, ensuring coherence between reason and revelation. It considers these as the basis for interpreting phenomena, including contemporary ones, through deduction and jurisprudence. Based on this principle, we see that Islam, in defining the motives of volitional action, is based on the following considerations:

a) Human beings are not merely biological structures driven by materialistic needs without limits, dictated by natural necessities. Rather, they consist of both body and soul, where the body's requirements are limited to the necessities of survival while the soul's requirements are linked to beliefs that integrate the motives of volitional action within the context of both the worldly life and the hereafter. In other words, the spiritual connection to the doctrinal dimension reflects a specific behavior for the individual, preventing desires and passions from dominating their pursuit of satisfaction. Instead, it aligns their motives with a system of values and virtues they embrace. The goods and services they seek are thus specific requirements for their existence as part of the context of life and not the entirety of life itself.

b) The spiritual dimensions of human beings are governed by a lifestyle oriented toward their perfection. This lifestyle makes their pursuit and pattern of life governed by the principles of virtue, moral elevation, and a system of values. Therefore, the utility does not find any elements to make it the standard of good and evil. Instead, good and evil are intellectual concepts defined by numerous social, ideological, and life circumstances.
c) Human beings, in their balanced psychological composition, require harmony between their sensual and desirous impulses, intellectual strength, and anger. Therefore, Islam, in its Sharia, promotes a lifestyle based on moderation, thus limiting spending on consumption to a level of sufficiency, as stated in this Quranic verse: "And do not make your hand [as] chained to your neck or extend it completely and [thereby] become blamed and insolvent."[162]

Based on these principles, and with acknowledgment of the importance of utility in human material life, it cannot be confined solely to the motives of one's pursuit in life. Rather, humans are on a continuous journey toward perfection, making virtue and the value system the actual driving force behind their worldly pursuits, which are linked to the world hereafter. Progression on the ladder of perfection leads individuals to engage in acts of goodness and sacrifice without expecting any benefit in return. Instead, they undertake noble and advanced actions, such as sacrificing themselves for the homeland, defending values, and protecting fellow countrymen without the slightest thought of the utilitarian returns from such actions.

On the other hand, the difficulties in managing life's affairs may be part of the process of refining the soul toward perfection. We cannot accept the notion that an action generating pain is evil and that everything leading to personal benefit is good. Therefore, within the principles of Islamic thought and its doctrines regarding self-assessment and progression toward perfection, we encounter painful

162 Surah Al-Israa, verse 29.

confrontations and challenges to test the soul and its resilience in facing specific painful actions. This empowerment, endurance, and elevation are part of the divine methodology in life for the believer in Islamic thought. It surrounds them with divine mercy and rewards, as stated in this verse: "And We will surely test you with something of fear and hunger and a loss of wealth and lives and fruits but give good rewards to the patient."[163]

Indications of the soundness of this interpretation of human volitional motives can be observed in our contemporary world, particularly in Western countries governed by liberal systems. There is widespread adoption of a lifestyle pattern known as "volitional simplicity," which advocates for rejecting the frantic pursuit of material possessions and services for utility. Instead, it emphasizes the spiritual dimension and actions associated with it as the source of human happiness. American researcher Amitai Etzioni states, "The idea of reaching higher levels beyond material consumption has been a foolish goal since the beginning of industrialization... Cultural norms have created deeply rooted orientations towards post-materialistic values."[164]

The expansion of understanding of "volitional simplicity" can be found in the same source below, through a statistical and analytical survey conducted by the Forbes Foundation in America. The conclusions drawn by the mentioned researcher indicate that human volitional motives and the pursuit of happiness, along with the prevailing mindset according to "volitional simplicity," underpin the philosophy of spiritual life advocated by religion and as highlighted by contemporary historian David Shi.[165]

On the other hand, when pure personal interest is linked as the sole link to happiness, and with its connection to individual freedom according to the liberal concept, and in the absence of the concept of virtue, it will lead to the phenomenon of decay in human values and behavior. Contemporary American writer Patrick J. Buchanan

[163] Surah Al-Baquarah, verse 155.

[164] William Hale and Kenneth B. Taylor, *The Economy of the Twenty-First Century* (Distributed by the Center for Arab Unity Studies), 189–190.

[165] Ibid., 198.

presents the implications of this in his recently published book *The Death of the West.* He provides field observations through statistical surveys, documenting abnormal occurrences in human behavior in Western societies.

The collapse of the primary fundamental value in society, which is the family, the decline of religious and moral norms, the spread of deviant relationships among members of the same sex, the rise in the number of illegitimate children, the increase in drug addiction, and extramarital relationships are all indications of the society's decay. These have made personal interest the criterion for happiness, separating virtue and spiritual values from it. Through analyzing this tendency of behavior, we believe that the concept of freedom becomes shallow when linked solely to self-interest in the absence of virtue, and there is no existence of virtue without belief in heavenly values.

9.2 Teleology

It is very clear in the prevailing economic thought in societies around the world that the goal of economic activity is to maximize profit for the producer at the lowest possible cost, while consumers aim to obtain the largest quantity of goods and services at the lowest possible price. We discussed this aspect in the instrumental section of liberal thought. However, this context takes on a different direction in Islamic thought, where the instrumentality of economic activity revolves around the concept of justice. We have presented the concept of justice as a rational concept supported by Sharia in the first part of our book, as an absolute pillar of religious principles, coming directly after the belief in the oneness of God within the components of the fundamentals of religion. Here, we will present the practical concept of the instrumentality of economic activity as a worldly matter necessarily supported by the rulings of Sharia.

The foundation of justice within the economic realm revolves around the fair distribution of resources. The practical scope to ensure justice in this context is based on two fundamental principles in Islamic thought: the principle of social solidarity and the principle of the community's right to public resources. The first entails satisfying the basic needs of individuals, while the second principle imposes broader satisfaction and a higher standard of life.

[In the third part of this book, we will return to the issue of resource distribution with more details and analysis. Here, we will only present the basic principles of the economic doctrine as absolute general rules.]

The contexts of applying the mentioned principles aim to promote societal equilibrium in the economic standard of living, as stated in the verse "so that it will not be a perpetual distribution among the rich from among you."[166] This is based on two truths, one existential and the other doctrinal, as articulated by Mr. Muhammad Baqir al-Sadr in his book *Our Economy*, as mentioned earlier. According to the author's affirmation, as previously cited in his book *Theses in Comparative Economic Thought between the West and Islam*, it is beneficial to summarize them here.

The existential truth. Human beings of the same species vary in different psychological, intellectual, and physical characteristics. There are differences in intelligence, inventiveness, and creativity, as well as in physical abilities. These variations among individuals cannot be explained solely by economic factors or any specific social context. The only justification lies in natural and biological factors, which are absolute truths and not merely products of a particular social framework.

The doctrinal truth. This stems from the principle of work as the basis for ownership. Consequently, the application of these principles allows differences in wealth among individuals based on their varying characteristics. However, Islam acknowledges that social balance must be understood within the recognition of these truths. Thus, it defines social balance as ensuring that wealth is distributed among individuals in a way that allows each person to live at a certain level rather than a complete contradiction in levels. This balance is the goal that the state seeks to achieve through various legitimate means

[166] Surah Al-Hashr, verse 7.

within its jurisdiction. To achieve this, control over the standard of living is necessary by both restraining excess from the top and uplifting those living at lower standards to a higher level. This ultimately leads to a general equilibrium in living standards. Sharia law has used the concept of wealth to achieve this balance by setting a clear distinction between the permissibility and prohibition of zakat in Islam. This boundary has been interpreted in texts using the term "ease" to facilitate the individual's livelihood to a level that aligns with the general living standard for people.

Hence, the first principle dictates that the state should provide the necessary conditions for individuals to live based on their work and efforts. If an individual is unable to do so due to any hindrance, the second principle comes into play, whereby the state implements social security measures through public finance to meet the individual's needs and provide a certain level of livelihood.

9.3 The tool

The proper functioning of a tool within the correct context is highly instrumental in achieving the goal. Economic life is undoubtedly a worldly matter that is inherently linked to its spiritual and ideological dimensions. According to the context we have discussed in this chapter, there are targeted values in worldly life specified by its tools, leading to two goals:

1) Justice, primarily economic justice, starts with distributive justice.
2) Balance between individual and communal life to serve development, progress, and meet the material needs of human life.

Based on this, the role of the individual alongside the role of the state emerges as pivotal, aiming for a state of societal justice conducive to human happiness.

Here, the human endeavor to possess wealth becomes evident, encompassing all its material components such as natural resources predating human labor, including land, minerals, treasures, water, and so forth. This pursuit extends beyond human labor to how these resources are utilized as raw materials or aids in the production process, culminating in the production of goods and services. Therefore, ownership, whether before or after the production process, determines the pattern of the targeted society.

In liberal thought, property ownership is derived from human freedom to acquire whatever satisfies their desires if it does not conflict with the freedom of others. Therefore, it is viewed in its context as advanced individual ownership, alongside any other form of ownership. This perspective contrasts with Marxist thought, which considers the individual as a part of the whole, not a composing part of it. Consequently, public ownership is advocated, considering its impact on the individual as the safest means to negate exploitation and to place the individual within the community as an inevitable context for development according to the historical materialism advocated by Marxism.

In the Islamic thought framework regarding property ownership, it is necessary to specify the following:

1) Ownership is a tool and not an end. It serves social and economic purposes to enable justice and create balance in society between individuals, others, and the community.
2) Since this ownership is a tool, it interacts with the economic and social realities existing in every society according to its historical development and progress. Consequently, judgments on economic phenomenon regarding ownership are based first on fixed principles (or what we previously termed as the "solid core") and second on the role of reason in analyzing the socioeconomic data according to the stages of societal development.
3) Since we are in this section of the study defining the Islamic economic doctrine, therefore, the rulings we define must be characterized by comprehensiveness and universality,

and through the analysis mentioned, we can reach the partial rulings and harmonize them with the existing data in society at its historical stage.

4) Ownership, as a tool, should target in its partial rulings derived from the comprehensive perspective, justice and balance in society between individuals, others, and social institutions, with the state at the forefront.

Based on these principles, Islamic rulings in their abstract comprehensive forms are according to the following context. Existence and its content are owned by the Creator, Almighty God, as stated in all contexts of Islamic thought. All ownership belongs solely to God alone. However, in the economic context of worldly affairs dealing with property, the ownership of Allah is a conceptual and legal matter. Humans are made trustees over it, and it is surrounded by standards and regulations that place it in the context of its purpose to serve faith and a just society. Therefore, it is a conceptual and legal matter, and its material existence in the worldly realm must serve the goal of justice and social balance by divine enlightenment embodied in Sharia and in harmony with the human intellectual trend in interpreting phenomena according to the existing societal data. Thus, the concept of ownership in Islamic thought, in its abstract doctrinal form, affirms the form of ownership in both individual and collective senses and the legitimacy of both private and public ownership.

Private ownership, in its essence, aims to satisfy the individual's needs to enable them to fulfill their existential mission in life while also delineating rights and duties in dealing with others in a just manner. Public ownership, in its various forms, serves as a tool for social balance, as stated in the Quranic verse "so that wealth does not circulate only among the wealthy among you."[167]

Here, the role of the state in the economy emerges, giving rise to a series of regulations and laws that serve this purpose, alongside partial rulings for individuals that specify their economic behavior, derived from both Sharia law and rational analysis of existing reali-

[167] Surah Al-Hashr, verse 7.

ties. While we are not delving into the analysis of the various forms of ownership recognized in Islam at specific historical stages, it is worth noting that they can be consulted when enacting rulings based on current economic and social variables. However, we are addressing contemporary Islamic political economy, which necessitates a separate section in our study to examine the legitimacy of economic analysis within modern Islamic thought. This section is essential for establishing general abstract rulings that apply to both the private sector in its various forms and the public sector, within the correct context of the state's economic role alongside its partial aspects. Through this approach, we become qualified to issue contemporary partial rulings addressing the economic life in our modern society.

Therefore, the cornerstone of ownership, within the framework of Islamic economic jurisprudence and its role as a driving force of economic life, revolves around the legitimacy of private ownership in its various forms and public ownership in its various forms, all supported by the role of the state in the economy.

In this general context, we move on to the specific context with its partial forms and its contemporary phenomena and data. These will not achieve their practical contexts and correctness if they are not associated with economic analysis capable not only of determining the legitimacy and correctness of governance but also correcting the vision for future actions that serve the desired economic policies for the development and advancement of society. This is what we will delve into in the third part of this study as it is imperative to elucidate the dimension of Islamic thought in its doctrinal form when applied in a partial context. Hence, it is necessary to derive partial rulings and address phenomena from a contemporary perspective.

9.4 Mechanism

The performance of economic operations and activities, within their general context, undoubtedly operates through the interaction of market mechanisms. Economic activity, whether concerning sellers and their freedom to enter or exit the market, or regarding goods, services, or labor force, operates according to the concept of freedom, as discussed in the first part of this study, reflecting the theoretical perspective in practical application. In its abstract and general forms, the market mechanism in Islamic thought is surrounded by standards and regulations aimed at justice and the elimination of exploitation based on two principles:

1) *Principle of self-determination.* This principle emphasizes the individual's self-definition, deriving strength and character from the spiritual and intellectual content of the Islamic personality. It acts as an internal barrier that prevents the individual, by their own will, from engaging in prohibited actions dictated by Sharia while adhering to permissible acts and fulfilling obligations that take detailed partial forms according to Sharia and reason.
2) *Principle of objective determination.* According to this principle, external forces, specifically the authority of Sharia, play a determining role, limiting personal freedom in activities conflicting with moral principles and goals deemed necessary by individuals. Sharia establishes boundaries to guide individuals by its abstract and general formulations.

The mechanism of the market, in its general form, operates within the context of competition, where a competitive market negates any influence on prices and quantities produced by a single producer or a small group of producers. It also prevents the ability to control the purchase of raw materials and impose a specific price. In other words, the market consists of many producers and establishments, and no single entity or small group can individually impact prices or production quantities. This concept of competition, which encountered another trend in the twentieth century as we discussed earlier in liberal economic thought, introduced the concept of monopolistic competition. In Islamic thought, the principle of dealing with this phenomenon is based on the avoidance of harm to individuals according to this principle: "no harm and no reciprocated harm; averting harm takes precedence over pursuing benefit, especially if the harm is certain, the benefit is individual, and the greater takes precedence over the lesser, and the essential takes precedence over the nonessential."[168]

The Islamic stance on monopolies is clear and explicit, as evidenced by the writings of the jurist Muhammad Hasan al-Najafi in *The Gems of Speech in Explaining the Laws of Islam* and in several other sources:

> Monopoly is forbidden in every kind for everything that respectable souls need and are forced to do, and for which they have no choice but to eat, drink, wear, or anything else, without being restricted by a period or by a period, or by a person without a person, or by a contract or by a limit, after assuming that the necessity has occurred. Rather, it appears that it will be priced at that time according to what is affordable for the seekers if the monopolist exceeds the limit in price. Rather, it is not far-fetched that it is forbidden to intend to cause harm due to high prices, even if people do not need it and things are abundant. Rather, it may be said that it is forbidden simply because of the intention and love of high prices, even if it is not to harm, and as a result, if monopoly is forbidden insofar as it is a general principle and a general rule, just like usury, for nothing else just because people need the monopolized thing, whether the need reaches the point of necessity or not.[169]

In addressing the effects of monopolies, Islam has legislated the intervention of the ruler, whether concerning the quantity of supply by compelling the monopolist alongside the supply that satisfies the

[168] Muhammad Jawad Mughniyah, *Imam Sadiq's Jurisprudence* (Ansarian for Printing and Publishing, 2000), part 3, 141.

[169] Ibid., reported from "gems of speech," 144.

demand or pricing according to what the ruler deems in the interest of both the buyer and the seller (i.e., imposing a fair price). This is indicated by what is mentioned about Imam Ali (PBUH) in *Nahj al-Balagha* and in several other sources regarding the concept of a fair price that balances between the producer and the consumer. This means covering costs and labor for the producer while satisfying the consumer's desire with what they should relinquish in cash for the desired commodity. Based on all this, Islamic thinkers, including Nasir al-Din al-Tusi, address the price as an estimate of the compensation at which the thing is sold, and it is not the price or the valued item itself. This is to negate exploitation in monopolies or the effects of supply and demand.[170]

The economic role of the state, the tendency embraced by neoliberal thought, especially among the newer liberals, completely contradicts what is advocated in Islamic thought, which emphasizes the important role of the state in the economic realm aimed at establishing justice, social balance, and public solidarity. The state intervenes in the market as a producer, owner, and distributor of natural resources in addition to its role as a regulator of market activity within the principles of freedom. This is done through institutions like regulatory bodies that work to ensure compliance with ethical rules in the market, prevent monopolies, and protect consumer rights. This takes its practical dimensions through economic analysis leading to a partial stance on phenomena and events based on existing economic and social data in specific times and places, all in line with the principles of Sharia and rational perspective, ultimately aiming toward a just society.

Other determinants in their abstract holistic form reflect their impact on the market mechanism through their partial applications derived from Islamic thought within Sharia. They possess a contemporary influential presence, such as usury (*riba*), which takes on the characteristic of absolute prohibition in its holistic form. Additionally, the illegitimacy of trading specific goods, such as alcohol, is found

---

[170] Nasir al-Din Muhammad ibn Hasan al-Tusi, *The Disclosure of the Intended in Abstracting Belief*, 321–322.

in detailed Sharia rulings, leading to specific objectives within the value system governing individual consumption behavior or even within the preservation of justice and societal security. Undoubtedly, addressing these issues will occupy an important space within the contemporary economic analysis of Islamic thought.

Our perception of the Islamic economic doctrine, in its totality and abstractness, cannot take on its practical dimension unless it is coupled with an economic analysis of contemporary economic and social data. It ensures the presence of principles in correcting the stance and implementing appropriate measures for contemporary economic phenomena by the harmony of Sharia and reason. This is what we will delve into in the third part of this study.

Part 3

Economic Analysis

Chapter 10

Introduction and Vision

Science is any type of knowledge that is the subject of conscious efforts that seek to develop it. Within this context, Alfred Marshall, an economics teacher at the University of Cambridge, believes that political economy, or economics, is a study of humanity in the practice of its ordinary life affairs.[171] Economic thinkers, in their methodology of dealing with economic thought and analysis, have established three axes for the contexts of economic thought:

1) The economic doctrine expresses beliefs, ideologies, and standards of what should be, comprehensively and abstractly, carrying an element of evangelism and preference. More importantly, it shapes the perspective through which economic phenomena are dealt with and their contexts analyzed. In the previous section, we presented our vision of the Islamic economic doctrine according to this context.
2) The economic analysis of economic phenomena aims to reach general governing laws of economic relationships, including theories, and also to understand the causality, dimensions, goals, or consequences of these phenomena and their governing relationship with other phenomena within the structure of the researched society. In its meth-

[171] Alfred Marshall, *Principles of Economics*, 8th ed. (London, 1920), 1:1.

odology, there have been divergent opinions regarding its validity, with some advocating for following the methods of the natural sciences and restricting it to physical experimentation. Meanwhile, others argue that both intellectual reasoning and experimentation are valid approaches. We will return to discussing this issue due to its importance within this section.

3) Economic policies or practical measures are derived from economic thought and analysis, ultimately leading society to a certain advanced state.[172]

Human efforts seeking knowledge create methods, approaches, and techniques to comprehend and control the phenomena discovered through these methods, surpassing the scope of empirical knowledge of daily life. Thus, science, as a field of knowledge, evolves its specialized methods for collecting data, interpretation, and deduction.[173]

However, the development of natural and applied sciences since the eighteenth century—based on the experimental and empirical method, which evolved under the hands of scientists like Newton, Galileo, and others—led to the restriction of the realm of acceptable scientific methods and the exclusion of others deemed unacceptable. This was in favor of the experimental and empirical method as an ideal model for all sciences. As a result, the term "science" became confined to knowledge that adhered to this method, as seen in physics and biology, because these fields claimed precision and certainty for their theories. Many classical philosophers and economists believed in this method in the realm of humanities and social sciences. They asserted that the validation of analysis and theories should follow the methods of natural sciences. Consequently, theories were formulated and tested within the framework of observation, statistics, and experimentation to prove their validity. This perspective was embraced by philosophers and thinkers such as Immanuel Kant, David Hume,

---

[172] John Kenneth Galbraith, *History of Economic Thought*, 8.

[173] Joseph A. Schumpeter, *History of Economic Analysis*, 1:31.

Charles de Montesquieu, Jean-Jacques Rousseau, Antoine Condorcet, Adam Smith, and others.[174]

It is very clear that the humanities and social sciences study human behavior, and economics is part of these social sciences. It is concerned with studying human behavior related to the production, distribution, and consumption of goods and services. This economic behavior includes the activities of individuals and groups, which are based on human will reflect in the human mind, and choices, and influenced by various social, cultural, technological, ideological, and logical factors. Meanwhile, the natural sciences investigate natural phenomena without human intervention and are confined to the quantitative aspect that is testable, aiming to reach specific quantitative judgments without any human influence or social, cultural, or ideological reflection by the researcher.

This contrast is not reflected in the methodology of dealing with phenomena. While the experimental approach in the natural sciences has proven successful and accurate, this does not imply that economists should adopt any method merely because of its success in another field. This is unacceptable, as contemporary liberal economist Hayek argues. Additionally, the structural and compositional variation of economic phenomena fundamentally differs from natural phenomena, which are formed independently of human influence. In many cases, economic phenomena are subject to deliberate human action and will, reflecting all the socioeconomic formation factors. If stripped of these factors, they would lack any significance, and their conclusions would be questionable. However, it is possible to subject some economic phenomena to the experimental method, but within a humanistic perspective that considers social influences. The primary concern in theories lies, for example, in the explanatory hypotheses as they represent essential components for statistical inference. The statistician must formulate a hypothesis about the joint distribution of random variables related to the phenomenon under investigation.[175]

---

[174] Hassan Agha Nazari, *Theorizing in Islamic Economics*, 83–84.

[175] Joseph A. Schumpeter, *History of Economic Analysis*, 1:41.

Here we present a striking example when we confine the validity of a theory to experimental methods alone. The theory of the logistic curve in demography, attributed to Pearl, starts from the assumption that living organisms are purely biological compositions, and their growth and reproduction are determined accordingly. Consequently, a series of tests are conducted on white mice in a laboratory to observe their growth, leading to the conclusion that their reproduction follows the logistic curve. This result is then generalized as an absolute rule applicable to humans! The hypothesis related to humans overlooks the socioeconomic and cultural formation of human beings, thus leading to a highly erroneous judgment. There is a vast difference between the growth of white mice in a closed laboratory and the growth of humans in an open society exposed to various socioeconomic, cultural, and ideological influences and so forth.

Based on what has been presented, we believe that reaching the validity of a theory and interpretive judgments will not be limited to experimental and empirical methods alone. Rather, intellectual efforts guided by socioeconomic, ideological, and logical influences play a significant role in deriving judgments and constructing theories or interpreting phenomena. This opinion is not solely based on the elucidation provided but also draws upon the views of the philosopher and Muslim scientist Ibn Sina, who argues that issues proven by reason or experience are genuine and not extraneous.

Islamic thought, based on divine enlightenment through legislation and teachings, grants a wide scope for reason in deriving contemporary judgments and interpreting phenomena. It views intellectual exertion as an open-ended process for dealing with emerging data through social evolution. Although it does not dedicate an independent domain under the title of economics, within the broader context of thought, it is rich with principles, judgments, and perspectives that facilitate the deductive process for generating interpretive judgments, theories, and understanding economic phenomena relationships. According to our perspective on the Islamic economic doctrine presented in the second part of this study, we see that this doctrine only takes its practical dimensions through economic analysis, which forms the perspective upon which the doctrine relies to build a worldly economic situation based on justice.

It is necessary to mention here a contemporary Islamic intellectual viewpoint that denies Islamic thought the capability of analysis, theory-building, and scientific interpretive judgments. Consequently, it denies scientific validity from Islamic economic thought, arguing the necessity of establishing an Islamic system through which we can explain phenomena. According to this perspective, we can't precisely interpret economic phenomena in Islamic society unless scientific studies gather empirical experiences.[176] Additionally, it states that Islamic economics cannot truly emerge unless it is embodied within the society's entity, rooted in its characteristics and details, and studied within organized economic events and experiences.[177]

Here are a few observations.

Islamic law, particularly in the economic field, presents both permissible and impermissible economic rulings aimed at regulating individual and societal behavior to achieve justice. Its rulings are directed toward all humanity, in harmony with reason. As mentioned earlier, scientific analysis fundamentally requires a comprehensive basis before the Islamic economic doctrine can be applied. The call to negate this possibility through the argument, by restricting the method that led to this conclusion to experimentation and empiricism alone, underscores the necessity of not confining analysis to this method. Isn't that the analytical approach, relying on deduction and ijtihad and drawing on Islamic jurisprudence, can arrive at scientific judgments in critiquing many economic phenomena under any economic system and it is conceivable that by following a scientific method can develop economic theories within the framework of an Islamic perspective?

We believe that scientific theorizing in Islamic economics, aimed at guiding individual and societal behavior and establishing justice within the context of applying the doctrine, is not only possible but necessary. This can be achieved through economic analysis and the extraction of theories and interpretative rulings to explain

[176] Muhammad Baqir al-Sadr, *Our Economy*, 334.
[177] Muhammad Baqir al-Sadr, *Our Economy*, 334.

the real relationships between economic phenomena and material and moral factors. Such an endeavor aims to guide the behavior of individuals and societies in our contemporary society, following an interpretative context in the field of economics that mirrors the context used in jurisprudence.

The third part of this study represents, through individual effort, an attempt at economic analysis from an Islamic perspective. Certainly, this endeavor alone may not fully meet the requirements of the subject, which should be addressed through scientific work by an integrated research team comprising economists, Sharia scholars, and Islamic jurists. Our work is a starting point on this necessary path. Within this context, I would like to mention the valuable insights provided by the economist Hassan Agha Nazari in his book *Theorizing in Islamic Economics* regarding the possibility of scientific theorizing in Islamic economics. He presents evidence, arguments, and data to conclude that "scientific theorizing in Islamic economics is possible."[178]

Our vision of the economy is not just a science seeking to maximize wealth, growth, capital accumulation, and increase in production rates of goods and so forth as much as it should be a tool for socioeconomic reform. At the forefront of this is justice in distribution and human development, meaning the restructuring of the social system; attitudes toward life, work, levels of education, and health; and the unleashing of the spiritual dimension of humanity. We believe that the intellectual path to presenting this concept will not be correct except through economic analysis stemming from the doctrine as a holistic perspective, capable of embodying the vision as an initiator for diagnosing the socioeconomic phenomena generated throughout the history of societal evolution, leading to the current contemporary situation. Therefore, the doctrine as a perspective is necessarily governed by the methodology of economic analysis if it seeks its doctrines, standards, and ideologies to have a place in practical application—meaning, more precisely, making theoretical wisdom a guide as a perspective for practical wisdom.

---

[178] Hassan Agha Nazari, *Theorizing in Islamic Economics*, 149.

Based on the above, the perspective emerging from the doctrine imposes methods and approaches in economic analysis. We have indicated and argued for the shortcomings of the empirical and positivist approach as an exclusive method for indicating the correctness of theorizing from its errors, and we have presented the rational approach without denying its empirical importance. For this method to take its dimension in analysis, it must have scientific tools and methods that we see in the following context:

1) The contemporary socioeconomic formation, with its developmental and historical effects, serves as data for diagnosing phenomena and influential variables, identifying the significant variable. As the variable condition resulting from development necessitates a context to follow, hence, building interpretative judgments must consider this context to ensure credibility, accuracy, and scientific integrity.
2) The use of statistics, especially in our present era of knowledge, which has brought about advanced technological tools, has greatly aided in enhancing the role of statistics. This is not only for interpreting phenomena but also for precisely understanding what needs to be interpreted.
3) When constructing theory, the focal point is established along with defining hypotheses, and a sound economic perspective presents standardized hypotheses. Here, the intellectual role of economic doctrine becomes apparent.

To illustrate the above, consider the following scenario. Classical economists at the end of the eighteenth and early nineteenth centuries believed they had achieved a concept of production factors and, consequently, the concept of value as fundamental pillars for understanding income distribution and thus wealth distribution justice. They built simplistic mathematical models based on this premise (known as Kozic's optimistic conclusions).[179] This trend, originat-

[179] Thomas Piketty, *Capital in the Twenty-First Century* (Economic Research Forum, 2016), 22.

ing from a capitalist doctrine based on natural law that supposedly adjusts the path of growth naturally without human intervention, failed to notice the issue of capital accumulation leading inevitably to wealth concentration and the denial of distribution justice. Twentieth-century statistics revealed the error of this trajectory by highlighting the phenomenon of income distribution imbalance in the world, as shown terrifyingly in the income distribution chart below, indicating the top 10 percent's control over roughly half of the world's income at the beginning of the twenty-first century:

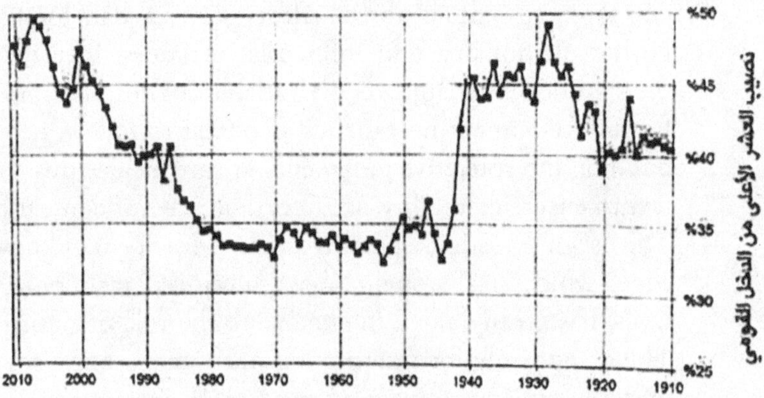

The share of the top ten percent of national income
Source: Thomas Piketty, *Capital in the Twenty-First Century*, 31.

Diagnosing the current contemporary situation with all its data and tools, if left to economic analysis stemming from the Islamic perspective of the doctrine and based on divine enlightenment and reason, would certainly view the situation from a futuristic perspective. When it sees the signs of the Almighty, there are flashes that the mind must grasp and enrich through economic analysis, indicating a divine enlightenment that places them so that wealth and riches do not become the privilege of the wealthy alone.

From this perspective, the third part of our study emerges, advocating a contemporary role for Islamic economic thought and political economy in our era. Its roots lie in Islamic sources in the Quran, the noble prophetic traditions, the teachings of the household of the Prophet, and the writings of Islamic scholars and thinkers, alongside reason and the application of our specific economic knowledge within its framework. It strongly emphasizes the necessity of establishing research teams, as we mentioned earlier.

Classical capitalist and liberal economic analysis have alternated within their scope since the late seventeenth century until today, involving numerous economists, philosophers, various schools of thought, and research centers. This capitalist analysis still constitutes a wide field for in-depth research and occasionally divergent trends but within the framework of liberal economic doctrine.

If we want the premises of Islamic economic doctrine to take on contemporary dimensions and possess a contemporary intellectual presence, Islamic thinkers and researchers must undertake extensive intellectual efforts. This includes the establishment of specialized scientific centers that give the required attention to economic analysis, enabling it to embody a global paradigm capable of occupying its rightful place, as envisioned by Islamic thought.

The scope of economic analysis is not limited to building economic theory alone. Rather, it encompasses various dimensions for analyzing phenomena, interpretive judgments on the causes and effects of economic movements, and the emergence of phenomena. It involves justifying the relationship between economic variables, the relationship of independent variables influencing the significant variable, providing the doctrinal perspective to the concept of existing phenomena and their crystallization, and so on.

Based on this, our approach in this part of the study, and through individual effort as we mentioned, will present models from an Islamic perspective, whether in the field of theories, interpretive judgments, or justification and causality of the dynamic interaction of economic variables and phenomena. We hope these models will stimulate a wide range of collective and individual efforts through Islamic research centers and thinkers as an obligation leading to fulfilling the divine message.

Chapter 11

Economic Theories from an Islamic perspective

11.1 The theory of factors of production

Our choice to start economic analysis with theories of factors of production and value was not coincidental. Rather, it was deliberate due to their fundamental role in economics, which reflects on phenomena such as distribution, inequality, prices, capital accumulation, wages, and production function, among others. These theories have occupied a central place in analysis among classical economists, liberals, and contemporary neoliberals. Therefore, our aim to provide a contemporary dimension to Islamic economic thought necessitates highlighting its perspective and vision on these fundamental economic theories as they constitute the appropriate and sound methodology to achieve our defined goal.

For illustrative purposes, we will initially address the theory of factors of production, not to prioritize it over the theory of value but for the sake of presenting the concept soundly as both are intertwined with overlapping concepts. It is also necessary to present them as theories according to what is stated in classical and liberal economic thought, followed by the Islamic perspective and its interpretive judgments. This presentation will take on absolute and abstract dimensions, devoid of spatial and temporal constraints.

11.1.1 Theory of factors of production in classical and liberal economic thought

The framework of the production process in its general context revolves around identifying the factors involved in the production process and their representatives, or in other words, the owners of these factors. Despite variations in the partial perspective among classical economists in describing and analyzing these factors, they generally follow the following approach.

A. *Factors.* These are determined by capital, labor, and land, which have been agreed upon among classical writers and were formally adopted by the economist Marshall.[180]

Adam Smith confirms the three factors as participants in the process of production and distribution. He deducts the shares of landowners and capitalists from the total product, which is entirely the product of labor. In other words, it is the recognition of labor alone as a factor of production. On the other hand, other views advocate presenting land and capital as factors of production to favor landowners and capitalists, as Ricardo did. However, it seems that classical economists, within the general context, leaned toward the tripartite scheme. This does not negate the views of some prominent writers among them who gave a prominent role to capital as a distinguished factor. Meanwhile, economist Senior spoke of capital as a secondary factor, as capital represents goods and thus raises the issues of depletion and renewal, which are problems not raised by other factors. As for the economist Mill, who spoke about land in this scheme, he referred to land rent, which enters or does not enter the price and cost, like how labor wages do, thus rejecting to place land on the same level as labor.

It seems that classical economists introduced a fourth factor added to the three factors, which is entrepreneur-

[180] Schumpeter, *History of Economic Analysis*, 2:251.

ship. Entrepreneurship involves hiring and combining other factors of production and is referred to as the organizer. It is considered one of the factors of production due to the mental and organizational work it provides in the production process in capitalist industry, replacing it with the capitalist who used to manage his businesses.

B. *Representatives.* They are the owners of these factors: landowners, capitalists who provide capital, workers who contribute to their labor force, and the organizer who is the entrepreneur, who, unlike workers, provides a different kind of effort. Among the classical economists who acknowledged this were Adam Smith and Cantillon, and Say says this: "The function of the entrepreneur is to organize the factors of production and transform them into a production apparatus." However, it is noteworthy that Ricardo and Senior completely excluded the role of the entrepreneur. But John Stuart Mill took a decisive step in using the term "entrepreneur" among English economists. When analyzing the function of the entrepreneur, he moved from mere monitoring to control, guidance, planning, and risk-taking.

C. *Distribution shares.* In contrast to the factors of production, the owners of these factors must receive their rightful shares. This includes rent for landowners, wages for workers, interest for capital owners, and profit for entrepreneurs. These distribution shares are justified as follows:

a) *Interest.* This is the portion of business gains that results from the use of physical capital, transforming financial capital into physical capital such as machinery, equipment, buildings, and the like. Here, physical capital takes on the context of enhancing production capacity and adding value. Therefore, net returns are generated from the use of this physical capital. However, this premise in classical capitalist thought did not meet unanimous acceptance. Hence, theories about interest emerged, and we will briefly present the most important ones:

Theory of interest in line with productivity. It stems from the fact that income is the price of productive services, which explains the return from capital goods, consistent with interest as the price of productive services provided by capital goods. There are divergent opinions on capitalist thought within this context. According to Ladoral in his specific definition of the productive role of capital, it is not "assisting labor" but rather a hint at the relationship between the substitutability of technological capital and labor, a step toward analyzing the relationship between wages and interest. On the other hand, James Mill and McCulloch argue that "capital profits are just another name for accumulated labor wages."[181]

Capital goods themselves are accumulated or stored labor, and what they represent in terms of labor simply continues to earn wages. Interest is what compensates for this additional work. Malthus, on the other hand, sees profits as fair compensation for the portion of production contributed by capital without specifying whether this return is interest or something else.

The theory of interest based on abstinence. Recognizing that capital is essential for production and that the net return generated by goods is equal to what is paid for the service provided by savings, the saver is the one who lends. They choose between the balance they should give up and the stream of interest they can obtain. Noticing different durations of capital turnover necessitates interest, which should equalize the returns of capital that complete their cycle and

[181] Schumpeter, *History of Economic Analysis*, 2:384.

recognize a certain element of abstinence or waiting. Therefore, interest is a "fair compensation" for waiting.

b) *Wages.* Wages theories also present varying perspectives, which can be summarized as follows. The subsistence theory of wages discusses the tendency of wages toward a necessary price to enable workers to live and reproduce without increase or decrease. The concept of subsistence level was replaced by Ricardo with the concept of "physiological subsistence level," which became known as the "social subsistence level." This refers to a quantity of essential items for life, deemed necessary for the sustenance of workers according to climate conditions and cultural habits, which dictates accepting wages based on this definition.

The theory of supply and demand by the English classical economists, described as the "wage fund doctrine," posits that at any given moment, there is a fixed number of workers available for employment, and there is no reserve wage at which workers would refuse employment. Conversely, the demand for labor is represented by a specific amount in real units that capitalists decide to spend on labor, and there is no wage at which capitalists would refuse to employ workers. Since the quantity of labor and the amount to be spent on it is given, and the quantity of labor demanded must equal the quantity of labor supplied for equilibrium, we obtain an equation that uniquely determines what is called the "average wage." When actual wages exceed this rate, unemployment becomes evident, and when they are below it, the demand for labor cannot be fully met. Hence, this theory is termed the "wage fund doctrine."

The marginal utility theory is one of the modern theories among classical capitalists. To determine the prices of factors of production and their distribution shares, we initially do not need to know their value based on utility. All we need to know are the consumers' preferences, the technological production conditions, and the initial distribution of factor ownership. Then the principle of maximizing net revenue, which includes the principle of minimizing costs, takes care of the rest. It is necessary to divide the utility value of the product among the factors exactly as the revenues from selling the product are divided among the factors. Therefore, the hypothetical process explains the actual process.[182]

Consequently, the rate of cash wage for each type of work, at perfect equilibrium under perfect competition, equals the modern material increase in production, attributable to the last increment of labor employed (marginal product of labor), multiplied by the equilibrium price of the product.

c) *Rent.* This is the portion of the land's output paid to the landowner for the use of the original and nondepletable powers of the soil, as defined by Ricardo. Rent, like other economic concepts, has undergone theoretical variations among classical and liberal thinkers, and we highlight the most important ones here:

   i. The theory of monopoly associated with Adam Smith reveals that landowners do not form cartels, nor are land services priced according to monopolistic principles. Instead, what is meant is that rent constitutes a situation regarding the pricing of scarce resources that exist in limited quantities.
   ii. The theory of diminishing returns associated with Ricardo, in one aspect, relates to rent,

[182] Schumpeter, *The History of Economic Analysis*, 3:247.

known as "differential rent." The question arises: Does it enter the price or not? Ricardo excluded it through the analysis of the varying costs of land parcels to conclude that in a state of equilibrium and perfect competition, the price cannot be lower or higher than the average costs of the most expensive facility. Thus, the true value of a commodity is regulated by the real difficulties faced by the producer under the worst conditions. Any additional increase in output is attributed to the increase in the total cost of production that must be borne to produce it. When there are diminishing returns, there is always an element of the product produced without any differential advantages. There are no permanent differential advantages for material factors except for the differential advantages of location and land fertility.

iii. Malthus's theory of production assumes that rent is a surplus attributable to the bounty of nature. Land can produce what is necessary to support the labor employed on it, and production is distinctive in that its expansion creates additional demand for its products because an increase in food implies an increase in population.

iv. As for the perspective of marginal utility, it sees rent as simply a matter of pricing the services of production inputs and applying the marginal principle to determine these prices. Natural factor rents tend to equal the value subtracted from their marginal products.[183]

[183] Schumpeter, *History of Economic Analysis*, 3:268.

d) *Profits.* The classical economists considered the organizer as one of the factors of production who hires or combines other factors of production. The profits of the organizer stem from the realization that the role of the capitalist, who managed his own business, was marginalized within the capitalist industrial system and was placed in a more suitable position among the owners of factors of production that are rented out. Thus, the organizer was added to the production process.

At the end of this presentation of the theory of factors of production among the classical and liberal economists, I see no need to repeat its details or discuss its developments as it relates to the overall perspective reflected by the doctrine. Therefore, the context of criticism will be addressed through our presentation of the concept of the theory of factors of production from an Islamic perspective in the following section.

11.1.2 Theory of factors of production from an Islamic perspective

While Islamic thought did not categorize its data and subjects under the title of economics, within the contexts of its presentation, it carries important elements that, if subjected to analysis and extraction of their depths, lead to the crystallization of an economic perspective characterized by depth and authority in sorting interpretative judgments and directions for theories that find their presence in our contemporary reality. In this section, in our approach to analyzing these data, we find a rich spectrum of profound insights that explain the production process and its factors, not merely as a descriptive case of the apparent but rather in its backgrounds, heights, and goals. We will provide evidence for this according to the following context.

In various Islamic intellectual works, we find the Islamic perspective addressing the process of generating action leading to the production of goods or services accompanied by a precise definition of each of its operations and indicators. We find this in the works of Ibn Sina in *The Metaphysics of the Healing* and in the writings of Sadr al-Din al-Shirazi in *The Transcendent Wisdom*, as well as in the works of Nasir al-Din al-Tusi in *The Abstract of Beliefs*. This perspective is particularly evident in the works of Ayatollah Sayyid Muhammad Husayn Tabatabai in *The Beginning of Wisdom*. Drawing on the data of these topics, we will present an overview of the production process coupled with precise definitions of its material existential concepts within a contemporary perspective.

Things exist fundamentally not by our choice and action, while others exist by our choice and action. Existence is divided into two categories. One is what exists in something else, that thing being ontologically independent and of the same type within itself, not as a part of it without contradicting its essence, meaning its existence within itself is itself the existence of that thing.

In my opinion, this limitation is unnecessary without saying "not as a part of it," and this category of existents is designated by the term "attribute," which is what exists in the subject. The second is what exists without being in something else in this manner, meaning it is not located at all, and this is designated by the term "essence."[184]

With perhaps a clearer presentation for easier comprehension, every possible existence is either existent in a subject, which is its essence, or existent in a subject, which is the accident. By the subject, we mean the place that subsists by itself and in which things are situated. This subject is either subsistent or subsistent by another, as there is a necessity for one to need the other. The first is called the substance, and the second is called the subject. In the first, subsistence is called form; and in the second, it is called accident. Substance and subject share a particular relation under the broader category of subsistence. The subject is more specific than the place, and particularity is broader than generality. Anything not situated in a subject is not in a subject and does not manifest. Hence, it is permissible for some accidents to be subsistent in others. Since the definition of an accident includes the probative condition presented in the division of substance, it is permissible for it to be included in the substance.[185]

---

[184] Ibn Sina, *The Metaphysics of the Healing*, 1:209.

[185] Nasir al-Din al-Tusi, *The Disclosure of the Intended in Abstracting Belief*, 2:728–730.

The existence of things includes those with the capability or potential to influence others, whether they are substances or accidents and whether they possess will or not. This potential is called "power." For example, heat is a power because it affects other things, as well as essential nature if it moves itself with natural movements or other movements (forced). Things have the power to act and cause something else to occur. Therefore, we say that a white cloth has the power to become black, meaning it has the potential to become black. So the thing whose existence is potentially possible according to reality is termed "existent by capability." As for something with the inclination and potential for action, its existence is termed "actualization," and the attribution of action in this sense to power is a complete attribution rather than an incomplete one.[186]

The Islamic thought, in its interpretation of the existence of things, attributes it to the principle of causality. "Cause" is the thing that results in the existence or nonexistence of another thing, and that on which the existence of a thing depends is impossible without it, and its existence is not necessary.[187] This is called effect. The sequence of causality to infinity is impossible as it ends with the cause of causes, which is God Almighty. Therefore, it can be said that everything originates either independently or as an addition. Hence, it becomes the cause of that matter, and the matter becomes an effect of it. If we assume the emergence of something from another, the emerging thing is an effect, and the emergence from it is a cause, whether the emergence is in the form of independence (as in perfect causality) or in the form of addition (like the part of the cause). If the part of the cause is something that results in another matter but not independently, then it is included in the limit.[188]

Based on the above principles, every temporal event is preceded by the power of existence. Before its actual existence, it must be possible for it to exist. It may exist or not exist, as if its existence were necessary, and its realization would be impossible. Likewise, if it were

[186] Ibn Sina, *The Metaphysics of the Healing*, 2:728–730.
[187] Ibid., 2:991.
[188] Nasir al-Din al-Tusi, *The Disclosure of the Intended in Abstracting Belief*, 96–97.

necessary, it would not fail to exist, but it might not exist. This possibility is not dependent on the ability of the agent, as the possibility of its existence is a description of it relative to its existence, not relative to something else like the agent. This possibility is external, with no conceptual meaning after the essence of the thing. The essence stands on its own and is apparent; it is a power and a material subject. Therefore, for every temporal event, there is a preceding material carrying the power of its existence—an actual power within it, not just a possibility. This is the power of things, and thus

1) every temporal event has a material substrate carrying the power of its existence;
2) the existence of temporal events is inevitably subject to change, whether in their manifestations (if they are essences) or in their origins (if they are substances);
3) power always acts, and matter always takes a form that realizes it—thus, if form follows form, the new form replaces the old, and matter persists;
4) power precedes action temporally.[189]

One of the necessities of a thing's transition from potential to action is the occurrence of change in the conditions of itself, and change is either impulsive or gradual (i.e., movement—the thing changes gradually).[190]

Therefore, there must be a mover, which is unmoved. If the mover itself possessed movement, it would necessitate that there be one thing both active and capable from one perspective, which is impossible. The essence of action is the essence of existence, and the essence of acceptance is the essence of loss. It makes no sense for one thing to be both existent and nonexistent from one perspective.[191] If something had movements of its own, its stillness would be impossible, as what is essentially stationary remains stationary. The sub-

[189] Muhammad Hussein al-Tabatabaei, *Explanation of the End of Wisdom* (Arab History Institute, 2015), 151–153.

[190] Ibid., 153.

[191] Muhammad Hussein al-Tabatabaei, *Explanation of the End of Wisdom*, 156.

sequent corruption necessitates the corruption of the antecedent.[192] Therefore, the mover is the cause of motion in the transition of a thing from potentiality to actuality.

Here, the discussion returns to things that exist by our will, as we indicated at the beginning of this passage. A human being does not produce an external action or movement intentionally unless its origin arises from within oneself. It passes through all its levels and powers that lie between the self and the appearance of its actions and the mechanism of its movement. Initiating action and movement from within oneself requires knowledge, which is the conceptualization of that action and belief in its benefit. Then it requires will, determination, honor, and a tendency to achieve it.[193] Therefore, it is the cause of movement from force to action.

The above presentation constitutes the Islamic perspective on the criteria and determinants of the production plan. Therefore, the context of defining the factors of production, their representatives, and the distribution shares comes with a contemporary vision according to the following formulations.

Factors of production. The concept of factors of production from an Islamic perspective is defined by the power or capability that brought about the production of goods or services. Thus, it is centered on the cause of the existence of the product from which the power transferred to action—namely, the material existing with the force gradually moved to produce the product. Consequently, the existence of the product is limited to the raw materials of production. Additionally, the existence of the product is also determined by the cause of the movement that transferred the cause of existence from the force to the action. Based on this, representatives of this performance are identified as factors of production, and beyond that, their participation in the production process does not exceed assistance without transitioning to the level of the factor that brings about the product.

The context of the production process progresses with the sequence of its performance from the perspective of the producer

---

192 Sadr al-Din al-Shirazi, *Supreme Wisdom in the Four Journeys*, 1:574.

193 Ibid., 2:610.

or organizer in our contemporary setting, who possesses the will according to a specific intellectual perspective. They undertake the task of gathering the production requisites to integrate within the framework of the production process, leading to the existence of the product. It begins first with the borrowing of financial capital. Here, it's worth noting that the first step in the production process, starting with financial capital, acknowledges the principle that money does not generate money (a notion acknowledged by economists since ancient Greek times), and it remains a valid truth. Money has a conceptual form to facilitate exchange, preserve value, and enable deferred payment. It does not possess any active material attribute in any production process.

Therefore, financial capital is transformed into commodity and service capital—namely, fixed capital (machinery, equipment, etc.) and variable capital (wages for workers and prices of raw materials). Through these, the production process takes place. As presented above, the existence of the produced commodity or service depends on the cause of existence and the cause of movement. The cause of existence is confined to the raw material that moves from force to action, thus constituting a factor of production. The cause of movement is associated with labor, whether physical or intellectual, making it a factor of production as well. Their representatives are the only factors of production entitled to value added or profits generated from the production process.

Fixed capital, such as machinery and equipment, are not causes of existence but rather auxiliary means. They are facilitators that bring the material closer to the actualization of action, similar to the movement of a moving object within each boundary of distance, bringing it closer to reaching its destination. They aid in materializing the event.[194] Thus, their absence does not negate the actuality of the event's occurrence.

The changing capital expressed in wages for labor and the prices of raw materials, the producer or organizer who transforms financial capital into commodity and service capital performs the price

[194] Muhammad Hussein al-Tabatabaei, *Explanation of the End of Wisdom*, 111–112.

payment operation to the owners of raw materials and ensures their price in determining the price of the produced commodity. In agricultural production, the land is a specific factor of production with the strength of the soil that transforms seeds into an action or fruit of the agricultural process.

Based on that, the perspective of Islamic thought derived from the contexts we presented confines the factors of production to labor in its physical and intellectual aspects, land, and raw materials for production. Their representatives have the right to participate in the distribution of the value added or the profit generated by the production process, where their determination is specified as follows:

- Financial capital is not entitled to participate in profits and therefore to earn interest. It deserves a wage for the loan it provides to the producer or organizer, whether there is profit or not. Similarly, fixed capital represented by machinery and equipment acts as an auxiliary factor, and its wage is implicitly guaranteed in the product price, and it is not entitled to profit sharing.
- Labor, as a production factor, has the right to participate in profits through its wages, whether physical or intellectual labor.
- Raw materials, whose price is guaranteed in the product value as production costs, and their returns belong to the producer or organizer.
- Based on this, the factors of production are determined by labor, wages, and profit sharing, as well as the intellectual and organizational work of the organizer or producer, whose returns are distributed accordingly.
- Land as a production factor has its returns.

11.2 Value theory

In my book published by Dar al-Balaghah in Beirut in 2015 under the title *Theses in Comparative Economic Thought between the West and Islam*, I addressed the concept of value both in the terms of

Western classical thinkers and in terms of Islamic thought. Revisiting the topic in this book is not a repetition of what was previously presented but rather an affirmation of the importance of the subject, with modifications, additions, and perhaps corrections to some of the previously discussed points.

The theory of value holds a central position in economic thought as it aims to identify the factors that explain ownership of something due to its value, and it regulates and governs value. The fundamentals of value analysis, with its roots in the scholastic tradition, will be discussed in line with the context of this work. We will explore the most important theories that have addressed value from that period up to the new liberals. Due to the impossibility of encompassing the vast amount of literature in this field, we will suffice with important milestones that constitute a framework for the evolution of the concept of value, followed by an exposition of the Islamic perspective on value. Before delving into that, it is necessary to clarify the concept of value as presented by classical writers in all stages. There has been a distinction between two concepts of value:

1) *Use value.* This refers to the utility that a person derives from consuming a particular good.
2) *Exchange value.* It signifies the quantity of goods that can be obtained in exchange for relinquishing one unit of the goods held by an individual. Exchange value is the value of concern in all the writings that will be mentioned.

11.2.1 Value theory among Western classical economists

Italian writers since the sixteenth century were the first to address the concept of value. Davanzati (1588) was the first to tackle the puzzle of value. He argued that while there are several essential goods like water with little or no exchange value, less useful goods like diamonds have a high exchange value, introducing the element of utility in the pricing process. This realization was acknowledged by the classical economists after a century and a half. Another Italian, Galiani, defined value as a self-equalizing relationship between a quantity of a certain commodity and a quantity of another commodity, determined by utility and scarcity.[195]

The resulting price determines the quantity that consumers can obtain, meaning it influences demand and is influenced by it simultaneously, leading him to discover the concept of equilibrium. Through this analysis, and surprisingly, Galiani shifts from scarcity to labor, describing it as the sole factor of production and the sole condition for all value, making equilibrium value proportional to the amount of labor.

Perloin's writings (1730) later formed the concept of commodity utility, known as marginal utility. The significance of an additional dollar for a particular individual is inversely proportional to the number of dollars they possess. If this is tied to income, then this additional dollar becomes known as the marginal dollar, and the utility derived from its expenditure is called marginal utility.

Adam Smith, through his famous book *The Wealth of Nations*, searches for price in a sense identical to value. He explains that wages, rent, and profit are the sources of all revenues derived from exchange value, and thus his theory of value is formed through costs (the cost of production) and is known as the theory of the cost of production. But elsewhere in *The Wealth of Nations*, Smith talks about a theory of value based on work, where it is stated that the true price of anything is what anything costs to a person who wants to obtain it, which is the effort and hardship required to obtain it.[196]

Hence, he returns to propose another concept of work, other than fatigue and hardship, but rather the quantity of work. Here we find this text: "Labor is the only thing whose own value does not change, and it is the only one that represents the ultimate and real measure of all commodities, or rather, its real price, or it is the only general and accurate measure of value."[197]

Ricardo (AD 1772–1823), who built his theory of value based on the work of Adam Smith after his extensive analysis of the data

---

[195] Schumpeter, *History of Economic Analysis*, 430.
[196] Ibid., 440–441.
[197] Ibid., 442.

in *The Wealth of Nations*, arrived at his central theory of value: "The exchange value of commodities under conditions of perfect competition is proportional to the quantities of labor embodied or incorporated in them, and this embodied labor truly represents the basis of all exchangeable value for all things."[198]

The neoclassicals brought about what is termed a revolution in value theory, transitioning to a classical model that stabilized around the year AD 1900. The revolution focused on the emergence of the theory of value based on marginal utility and was associated with the names of Jevons (AD 1835–1882), Menger (AD 1840–1921), and Walras (AD 1834–1910). The essence of what the neoclassicals concluded can be outlined in the following manner.

Different categories of needs, goods, or desires define the concept of commodities and can be arranged in a specific hierarchy of importance (self-interest). Within each category of these classifications, there is a given psychological fact, a specific context of desires to achieve additional increments from each commodity felt whenever we continue to consume successive increments of the commodity.

Based on this, the law that formed the basis of the new psychological theory of value is proposed. As we consume successive increments of each commodity, our desire for an additional unit of it decreases steadily until it reaches zero. Based on this, the law is formulated as follows: "The marginal utility of anything for any individual diminishes with every increase in the quantity he has of it already." As for total utility, as a sum or integral, the total utility of anything for any individual increases to a point of saturation with each increase in it, but at a diminishing rate. The second law is stated as follows: To ensure maximum satisfaction from any commodity capable of satisfying different needs, individuals or institutions should allocate that commodity to different uses in a manner that equalizes the marginal benefits in all these uses. Their interpretation of exchange value falls within the realm of use value, which was previously rejected by Smith and Ricardo. The essence of this new theory of exchange lies in the analysis of marginal utility, which has created an analytical tool appli-

[198] Ibid., 298.

cable universally to economic problems. The concepts of marginal and total utility refer to consumer needs, meaning they only carry direct meaning about goods and services that satisfy consumer needs.

But Singer asserts that means of production, or goods of higher order (as he calls them), fall within the concept of economic goods because they also indirectly satisfy consumer needs by aiding in the production of goods that directly satisfy consumer needs. This perspective treats items such as iron, cement, natural resource services, and labor as incomplete consumer goods, broadening the scope of the principle of marginal utility to encompass all areas of production. That is, inputs and factors of production acquire utility value through which they gain indicators of their economic importance and thus their exchange value from the same principle of marginal utility that provides indicators of economic importance. Consequently, it explains the exchange values of consumer goods. However, these exchange values or relative prices of factors constitute production costs for the producing firm. This means that the principle of marginal utility now gives rise to the phenomenon of cost and the logic of resource allocation (production structure), and thus the supply side of the economic problem, as much as all this is determined by economic considerations. On the other hand, we look at the relative costs for the firm as inputs for households. Thus, the principle of marginal utility, with the same condition, automatically covers the phenomena of income formation or distribution. Thus, all elements of the economy converge to research based on one principle.

11.2.2 The theory of value from the Islamic perspective

It's quite clear from our discussion of Islamic economics that justice holds a prominent position within it. At the heart of justice lies the Islamic perspective on value, which emphasizes fairness for both consumers and producers alike. This aligns closely with what we presented in the previous section regarding the factors of production and our focus on the elements generating added value. Through the intellectual frameworks of Islamic thought, the Islamic perspective on value emerges. To begin with, it's essential to clarify fundamental concepts that serve as contemporary fundamental determinants.

We present a manufactured commodity according to modern manufacturing, produced in a facility using equipment, machinery, raw materials, buildings, and labor. Consequently, the production of this commodity incurs costs and labor, embodying both in its existence. Thus, the commodity derives its value from itself, encapsulating both the costs and the labor. In other words, this commodity has acquired a real value, expressed monetarily, equivalent to the costs incurred and the labor invested. It can be exchanged for another commodity whose costs and labor are balanced. It now has absolute real value, whether it is sold in the market or not. For the producer, this value represents the minimum price required to cover costs and labor. If this minimum is not met, producing the commodity becomes meaningless as selling it at a lower price would result in unfairness in pricing. Therefore, commodities possess real or absolute values regardless of the selling price, which varies from one market to another based on supply and demand, timing, location, and other influencing factors.

Here, Islamic thought distinguishes between real value and price, whereas in Western thought, these are often considered synonymous without differentiation. This can be observed in the writings of Western economics and liberal thinkers. What is referred to as exchange value in perfect competition, and in our current era dominated by money, is nothing but the price. It is determined based on the effects of supply and demand—on the supply side by the minimum threshold according to costs, labor, and profit margin, and on the demand side by the purchasing power provided by the utility derived from the commodity for the consumer.

In terms of intellectual foundations related to value, the Holy Quran and Islamic sources, as referenced earlier, emphasize the praise of work, particularly work combined with proficiency. In the teachings of Imam Ali (PBUH) and in various Islamic texts, the concept of fair price, which equates the producer with the consumer, is extolled. This means that the price covers the costs, labor, and profit margin for the producer while satisfying the consumer's desire with what equals their payment in exchange for the desired goods. Through these concepts, the real value aligns closely with the prevailing market price. This perspective is also echoed in the theological abstraction by al-Tusi, where he distinguishes between price as compensation for selling something and value or worth.[199]

Based on the above, we can define the Islamic perspective on value and offer a contemporary view as follows.

Goods have inherent real value embodied in them through the costs and labor expended in their production. These values are absolute regardless of whether they are offered in the market or not.

The price of goods is determined according to the supply of real value at its minimum and demand through a combination of factors, including purchasing power availability and supply-demand balance, resulting in variations from one market to another.

From an Islamic perspective, fair pricing is determined by the proximity of the price to the real value. The closer it gets, the more just it becomes. Matching the price with the real value constitutes the equilibrium price in a perfectly competitive market. According to this formula, real forces are formed to prevent any inflation that may harm justice.

The value of labor is not only determined by the number of hours worked but also by the quality, level of education, and training of the workers.

As for the standard formula for value, based on the above, it is as follows:

$v = x + LRn$

Where:

v = Value

x = Costs

L = Rate of labor to produce one unit of goods

Rn = Rate of worker's wages at a specific educational level

[199] Nasir al-Din al-Tusi, *The Disclosure of the Intended in Abstracting Belief*, 321–322.

Where n can be a differential classification of educational and training levels, taking levels 1, 2, 3, 4, and within the time frame as an average to produce one unit of goods.

Therefore, this real measured value serves as a standard for justice when the price approaches it.

11.3 Demographics from an Islamic perspective

The validity of any theory depends on its foundational assumptions and the accuracy of the premises upon which it is based. The theoretical wisdom's implications are manifested in the interpretation of movements and their purpose, inevitably revealing their necessity. In other words, demographic issues are merely branches of the intellectual perspective of humans, considering their material and spiritual dimensions. The variations that have arisen in the perspective of humanity over previous periods have influenced the interpretation, causality, and goals of demographic issues. This variation has led to the emergence of different demographic theories, which diverge or converge depending on the perspective from which they originated.

And since we have addressed the concept of human beings in the first part of this book, it is necessary to recall some of the principles that have been presented, with just a few references without falling into repetition.

Before that, we point out the contexts of crystallization historically according to the perspective that governed the treatment of the population issue, which constituted one of the most important central topics over the ages and was viewed from different angles. Since ancient times, the population has been an issue. In ancient Chinese thought, the population issue was dealt with from the perspective of the great imperial state and was limited to the physical existence of the population and its reflection on the consolidation of the course of the empire. It included insights into population growth and its relationship to resources. They believed that excessive population growth leads to a decrease in the output of the average worker and thus a decrease in the standard of living of the population. As a result, it would create unrest and conflict. It is necessary to maintain the optimal ratios between population and economic resources, which is the responsibility of the state at the national level. They argued that high mortality rates are connected to a lack of food. Although they studied how populations move and interact with the environment, they did not suggest practical ways to balance population movement and available resources. Instead, decisions were based on the empire's interests, and the discussion lacked a comprehensive understanding of the concept of humanity.[200]

Greek thought dealt with the population issue from the perspective of a "civil state" and discussed opportunities to reach a virtuous life according to economic self-sufficiency and, at the same time, being able to protect itself militarily. According to Greek reality, Plato determined the size of the virtuous city at 5,040 souls—the population size for the demands of peace and war. We also notice that Aristotle and Plato encouraged the idea of birth control and their consideration of it as an essential part of rational population policy.[201]

As for Roman thought, it also viewed the population issue from the perspective of a great empire, advocating population growth for military purposes. Most of their practical measures were based on this specific objective.

During the Middle Ages, we only refer here to the ecclesiastical thought that addressed the population issue from literary and moral perspectives, without any concern for material and economic aspects. Overall, opinions leaned toward population growth, with condemnation of practices like abortion, divorce, and polygamy while advocating for chastity, purity, and preference for marriage.[202]

In our contemporary history, since liberal thought prevails in the largest number of countries in the world and their policies are based on the classical and liberal perspective of Western thinkers, and also that the demographic issue gained prominence with Robert Malthus (1766–1834) to become an important branch of social eco-

[200] Mohamed Kazem Al-Mouhajir, *Summary of Lectures on Population Theories* (Arab Institute for Training and Statistical Research), 4.

[201] Ibid., 5.

[202] Ibid., 7.

nomic studies, demographic policies—even the current economic policies that prevail in the international community—are based on the perspective of these thinkers and writers, which necessitates a brief presentation of the foundations and perspectives of this thought before discussing our view of the Islamic perspective.

11.3.1 The classical and liberal Anglo-Saxon thought

The Western classical perspective on population issues, as we mentioned, was influenced by figures like Robert Malthus. It precisely reflected the Western view of humanity as we presented it in the first part of this book. In its advanced stage, liberalism sees the embodiment of the Creator in the inevitable laws of nature, and it objectifies humans. Consequently, its perspective is confined to biological composition. Based on this, it explored population issues about population growth and its food and material needs, limited within this scope. And what emanated from that was nothing but paths that serve this trend to objectify man within his biological makeup and the material requirements of living for his continuity. Consequently, the population theories in liberal thought were confined to the balance between population size and growth on one hand and food growth on the other. Therefore, we will present examples of these theories along with their contemporary presence in the policies of Western countries and their dealings with the world, especially with developing countries.[203]

The general Malthusian theory on population, which was formulated by Robert Malthus, emerged in the environmental conditions surrounding the industrial transition in Europe. This was reflected in unemployment, urban expansion, and the widening supply of labor forces along with its impoverished social effects. Malthus formulated his theory based on two fundamental premises:

1) Food is necessary for human existence.

[203] P. K. Halatbari, *On Deportation in Development Slums* (Akademie-Verlag, 1968), 33–47.

2) Sexual desire is necessary and will remain so as long as the human race exists.

These are two truths that will not change throughout history. Malthus linked the production of food to land, emphasizing its limited capacity with the total area suitable for agriculture. The increase in food production depends on the addition of new agricultural lands, which is a finite resource. Increasing the productivity of cultivated land also has its limits as agricultural production is subject to the law of diminishing returns. Through statistics he conducted on American regions, Malthus concluded that if population growth is not regulated, it will increase exponentially:

Geometric sequence: 2-4-8-16-32-64...

Food production, under the best conditions, will increase according to a numerical sequence:

Arithmetic sequence: 1-2-3-4-5-6-7...

Based on this, after two centuries, the population-to-food ratio becomes 9/956. And after three centuries, it becomes 13/4,096. After years pass, the possibilities are endless.

After this presentation about the two basic hypotheses of his theory—namely, the necessity of food for human existence and the necessity of affection between genders for life—while the latter hypothesis leads to an imbalance between population and food, the law of need resulting from the first hypothesis restores this balance through the forces generated by this imbalance, which manifests in the increasing pressure of the population on limited life necessities. Malthus named these forces that lead to the necessary balance between population and food as population control. Here comes the treatment at the same level as other living beings according to the natural law they believe in. Malthus defined population control in two categories:

1) *Positive control*, which is the most effective in increasing mortality rates. And their fundamental characteristics are misery and sin, which humans suffer from as a result of their tendency to grow at a rate that exceeds their ability to produce life necessities. The components of this category include famines, epidemics, the spread of poverty, food shortages, and the prevalence of disease, as well as wars and various forms of imbalance.
2) *Preventive control* distinguishes humans from other living beings, working alongside births to reduce them in a way that helps achieve the necessary balance between population and food production. Their main characteristics include insight into the population problem, and their components are summarized in what he called "moral restraint," which encompasses abstaining from marriage or delaying it, practicing moderation, and self-regulation. This preventive control increases with the degree of civilization progressively. It is evident that as preventive control increases, positive control decreases, and vice versa. Malthus believes that the population principle, which entails the rapid increase in human numbers compared to food production, realistically requires the operation of positive control to achieve a balance between the two forces. They are indispensable, meaning accepting a degree of misery and hardship to reach the required equilibrium. Based on this premise, Malthus strongly opposes poor laws because they encourage irresponsible marriage and reproduction, weakening self-reliance, which may lead to the operation of positive control. Therefore, these laws must be abolished.

Malthus's theory has indeed stirred some panic among people and sparked numerous scientific discussions among economists, laying the groundwork for the development of population thought that has persisted until our contemporary era.[204]

It's no wonder to see the economist Senior (1829) incorporating a Malthusian doctrine into the basic tenets of economic theory, which leads to the following: "The size of the world's population, or in other words, the number of individuals residing in the world, is determined solely by ethical or natural guilt, and by the fear of scarcity in those resources of wealth that determine the habits of individuals of all classes and their needs from them."[205]

Perl's logistic curve. Based on the perspective we mentioned in Western thought, and considering the human being merely a biological structure subject to the deterministic laws of nature, Raymond Perl conducted experiments on insects and white mice in a laboratory and observed their proliferation. And after the specified period, and through mathematical operations, he reached the conclusion according to the results of his experiments that population growth proceeds according to a logistic curve, where the population is an independent variable that is subject to its biological law, and thus the world's population is multiplying according to this trend as he claims to have observed this through population growth in Western Europe.[206]

---

204 Mohamed Kazem Al-Mouhajir, *Summary of Lectures on Population Theories*, 128–132.

205 Schumpeter, *History of Economic Analysis*, 2:279.

206 P. K. Halatbari, *On Deportation in Development Slums*, 41.

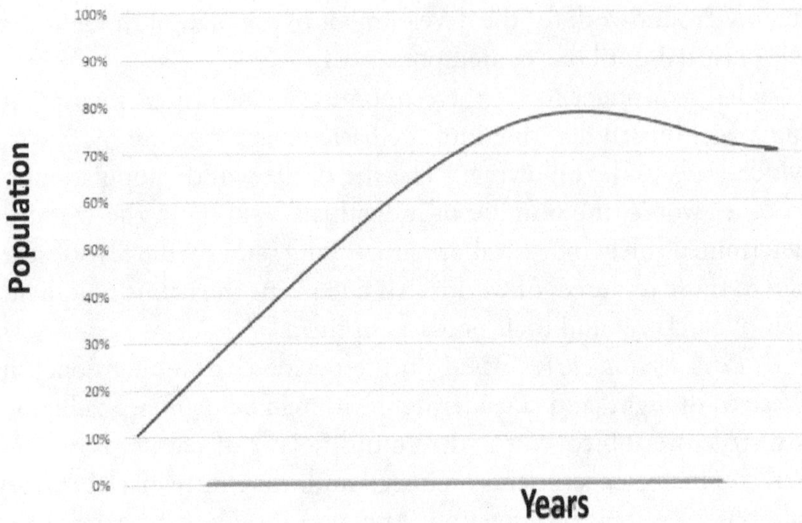

Perl's logistic curve

We don't need much effort to see that there is a vast difference between the growth of insects in a closed laboratory and the growth of humans in an open society with its material, spiritual, social, and cultural dimensions. But the essence of the issue lies in the premise that humans are mere biological compositions subject to the laws of inevitable nature.

The classical economists after Malthus

With a clear influence from Malthusian thought, the writings of Western classical economists generally painted a dramatic picture of economic growth under the influence of Malthusian population pressure. This can be summarized by the following graph, which illustrates the features of this picture:

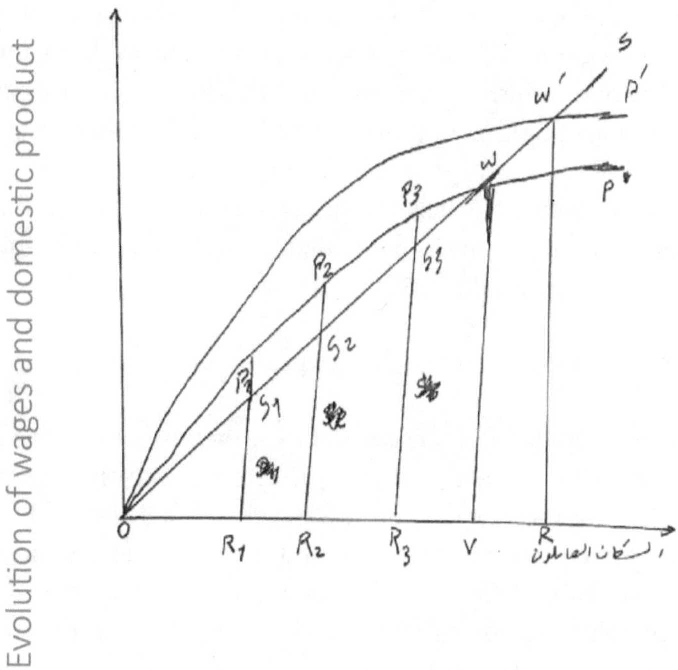

- Capitalist economy under population pressure as envisioned by the classics.
- Vertical axis: Development of wages and GDP (general domestic product) after deducting profits paid to landowners.
- Horizontal axis: Number of working populations.
- The central OS line represents the development of wages paid to workers, and it appears as a straight line because it reflects the idea of the subsistence wage, or the minimum wage believed in by classical economists.

If the number of workers is zero, then the wages paid will be zero. However, if the number of workers is 100 at the subsistence wage level, then the subsistence wage level can be determined as follows if we calculate the slope (OS) through the result of the ratio of VW, which is the result of dividing the wages paid by the number of workers (assuming OV equals 100 workers).

The curve (OP) represents the evolution of the size of the gross domestic product after profit payment. This curve starts from the origin, ascending upward from the top left to the top right until it takes a position parallel to the horizontal axis due to the assumption of the law of diminishing returns and their assumption of an increase in profit with population growth. If we assume the working population is OR1, we find that the size of the gross domestic product after profit payment equals the distance R1P1. Here, we find that the wages paid represent R1S1, while the size of the surplus or profit remaining for capitalists is this:

Profit = Gross output - Wages paid = R1P1 - R1S1

If the population increases to OR3, then the size of the output becomes R3P3. From this size, capitalists pay wages amounting to R3S3, leaving them with a surplus equal to S3P3. From the graph, we observe that the size of wages paid begins to increase noticeably due to the rising prices of agricultural goods, leading to an increase in profit, while the surplus or profit decreases significantly. However, capitalists continue to invest if the profit rate does not fall below the acceptable level that stimulates investment.

If the number of working populations reaches OV, we find that the size of the output has reached VW. However, at this level, we find that wages have begun to consume the entire size of the output (after profit payment), causing profits to disappear completely and the profit rate to become zero. There is no surplus allocated for investment. Consequently, economic growth stops, and the system enters a state of stagnation and recession.

If we assume that technological advancement will increase productivity levels and thus the size of output, the classical economists regarded the effect of this factor as temporary. It could delay the national economy to the point of recession, but it was not conceivable that it would prevent reaching this point. Therefore, a curve for the development of output (OP) could be envisioned, which rises above the old curve to indicate the impact of progress in increasing productivity levels. Here, we find that all that has happened is that the new recession point (W) has shifted to the right of the old recession point. In this case, technological progress would increase the capacity of the national economy to support an additional population of approximately VR. However, economic growth thereafter becomes impossible due to the absence of profit and, therefore, the absence of capital for investment, leading again to recession and the inability to support any additional population.[207]

While Malthusian thought and its ramifications have faced wide scientific criticism despite the intellectual trend it follows, the pessimistic trajectory of this thinking and the imprints of Malthus continue to extend their influence into our contemporary times. They constitute a fundamental factor in population policies and even in difficult, inhumane decisions. Here, we refer to the Forester law in the mid-twentieth century and its implications in this manner: "In complex situations, efforts made to fortify things often tend to make them worse, sometimes much worse, and occasionally turn them into a catastrophe." This means the transformation of humanitarian health aid to developing countries and the redirection of its course due to population growth![208]

But what is astonishing in our current reality is the extensive programs outlined by United Nations agencies (such as the United Nations Population Fund, the International Monetary Fund, the United Nations Development Program, etc.) in addressing the population issue through population control measures such as family planning. These approaches often blame the populations of develop-

---

[207] Mohamed Kazem Al-Mouhajir, *Summary of Lectures on Population Theories*, 29–31.

[208] Hal Hellman, *The Problem of Population Inflation* (Al-Maaref Publishing House, 1974), 27.

ing countries and hold them responsible for hindering growth and progress in the world due to their excessive reproduction.

11.3.2 The Islamic perspective

The goal of this book, as I envisioned it, is not to build theories characterized by comprehensiveness in the phenomena of existence. Instead, it aims to indicate the capability of Islamic thought directed toward all of humanity in analyzing and constructing theories within any economic system. Such a purposeful context for building theories in this way would not be an individual effort but rather an intellectual product characterized by collective work, research teams, and perhaps an accumulation of thought by economists who combine economic ability with a comprehensive understanding of Islamic thought. The population issue, as presented in the context of liberal thought, has been limited to the physical existence of humans according to the requirements of life without extending to human spiritual, intellectual, and even behavioral dimensions within ideological patterns. Since Islamic thought based on reason and revelation cannot be confined to this narrow scope, there must be a research methodology based on the issue of humanity in all its spiritual, intellectual, legislative, cultural dimensions, relying on beliefs and standard judgments alongside known sources, as we mentioned earlier, and enlightening jurisprudence with its determinants. The population issue is a derivative part of this context and not the subject in its entirety. Therefore, I decided that my next book, following this one, would be titled *Humanity and Demography in Islamic Thought.* Here I will present data and approaches from Islamic thought to indicate the capability of this thought to formulate theories characterized by depth and comprehensiveness in interpreting and justifying the existential phenomena related to humans. In line with the presentation of liberal thought, it will be limited to the population issue and not the human with all its dimensions as we have indicated.

The legislative aspects in Islamic thought and literature have not only addressed the population issue from ethical and literary perspectives but have always been linked to economic and material aspects, setting contexts and parameters for many demographic issues. Here, we refer to some of them.

Reproduction in Islam occurs solely through the institution of marriage, and any birth outside this institution is illegitimate and beyond the legally prescribed guidelines. Marriage has financial constraints (the amount of dowry given at the time of marriage and any additional payments), which are derived from the economic capability of individuals. Reproduction is tied to the ability to provide for the offspring, and the size of the family should be commensurate with the economic capacity of the provider. It is mentioned in a noble hadith: "In goodness, there is a scarcity of offspring, and in abundance, there is a sign of poverty." The solution for the pleasure of a married person, when economic capability weakens, is through the practice of isolation (temporary marriage) permitted by Islam or intermittent contact. Consistent with this context in the contemporary age, birth control methods serve as constraints for divorce, which have financial constraints (payment of a fair settlement and expenses during the waiting period).

In its legislation, Islam addresses humanity through its perspective based on human perfection, as mentioned in the Quran: "We have created mankind in the best form,"[209] and complete with the knowledge that is obligatory upon every Muslim, male and female. This means that guidance, wisdom, and insight are essential characteristics for the addressed human being within the fundamental framework of their existence, which is the family and society. They form a value system in behavior, ethics, and conduct, serving as beacons that define the path of life for individuals in their worldly realm. From this perspective, the size of the population, in terms of its existence in life and this universe, is defined and balanced. Departing from the constraints we have mentioned, as indicated by some of them, will lead to imbalance. "Has the abundance of wealth and children distracted you? Until you visit the graveyards?"[210] Neglecting the constraints, principles, and values that govern the approach

[209] Surah Al-Tin, verse 4.

[210] Surah Al-Takasor, verses 1–2.

and course of life will lead to an imbalance in reproduction and an increase in mortality rates.

As for the other aspect related to the issue of food, which has alarmed liberal theories around the world, Islamic thought and its doctrines lean toward another direction. First, they affirm that the occurrence of risks related to food scarcity is not inherent in things, but rather, they are the results of imbalances in the socioeconomic situation that lie in behavior. Here are some confirmations:

> There is no creature on Earth but that its sustenance is upon Allah.[211]

> And if you count the favors of Allah, you will not be able to number them.[212]

It is important to understand that natural resources exist in abundance and are available to humans without any deficiency. If there is an imbalance between population growth and the availability of natural resources, it is not due to their scarcity. The main cause of this imbalance is the unequal distribution of resources. Realistic statistics from many countries around the world have shown that the wealthiest 10 percent of the population controls 60 percent of the gross domestic product. Additionally, factors such as human behavior, perception of natural resources, and the accumulation of wealth are influenced by the actions of authorities through oppression and corruption. The quote "No poor person has ever gone hungry except due to what the rich have consumed"[213] reflects this imbalance.

As for the aspect of the mutual relationship between population dynamics and natural resources, we affirm that population is not an independent variable but rather contingent upon the surrounding environment, foremost among which are patterns of production and human behavior. Islamic thought has come to establish boundaries

---

[211] Surah Hud, verse 6.

[212] Surah Al-Nahl, verse 18.

[213] A noble saying of the Prophet Muhammad ﷺ.

and illuminate the path of human behavior. It emphasizes that human needs are not solely biological but fundamentally linked to social and cultural aspects that constitute motives alongside biological and psychological structures. Human needs are not solely determined by the natural biological demands of individuals or human communities alone, and these demands do not suffer from real scarcity but rather from misuse and inequitable distribution. The reference for this is the sociocultural context and the psychological characteristics of humans. Considering this, Islamic thought and its vision of human behavior address enlightenment from the divine perspective, aiming to regulate human behavior by gradually producing resources according to human scientific capacity and divine guidance.

> And if Allah had extended [excessively] provision for His servants, they would have committed tyranny throughout the earth. But He sends [it] down in an amount which He wills. Indeed, He is, of His servants, Acquainted and Seeing.[214]

Consequently, it offers guidelines for human economic behavior by presenting a practical approach to moderation in expenditure: "And do not make your hand [as] chained to your neck or extend it completely and [thereby] become blamed and insolvent."[215] And He forbids extravagance: "And do not spend wastefully. Indeed, the wasteful are brothers of the devils,"[216] thereby approaching the available resources and the requirements to satisfy needs, objectively setting a limit to the level of sufficiency.

After this presentation, can we not demonstrate the capability of Islamic thought in constructing a "population model" according to the dimensions of population size and growth, natural resources, and their dialectical relationship in human behavior in an Islamic society with its enlightenment, regulations, and legislation? Yes, it is

[214] Surah Al-Shura, verse 27.
[215] Surah Al-Israa, verse 29.
[216] Surah Al-Anaam, verse 141.

certainly possible to build this demographic model according to our vision as a society with a stable population with moderate population growth, abundant natural resources, and a prudent and rational approach to human behavior.

3. The economic analysis of contemporary phenomena is based, in its methodology and context, on the beliefs and standard judgments of Islamic thought, and according to the rational perspective.

What we have presented in the introduction of this third part of our work constitutes the fundamental perspective for dealing with economic phenomena in interpreting their causes, outcomes, or objectives. At the same time, the economic doctrine imposes a specific approach to this perspective, aligning theoretical vision with practical contexts on the ground. In other words, theoretical wisdom enlightens how to practically deal with issues, which is practical wisdom. Additionally, the doctrine mandates tools for dealing with issues within the framework, especially hypotheses and statistical data. For the analysis to be accurate according to Islamic thought, it is necessary to clarify a central and important issue, as follows.

Since the knowledge framework according to Islamic thought is based on both reason and revelation and since the legislator supports reason in its manifestations and the correctness of its path, we see that the rulings of Islamic law included absolute and unchangeable judgments, especially in areas of prohibition and analysis. This is what we referred to earlier and labeled as "the solid core." Alongside these fixed rulings, the trend of thought that believes in evolution in all its social, economic, and technological aspects and so forth, the generation of updated data within the economic framework imposes a deep intellectual and analytical effort on these existing practical data in a way that is consistent with the provisions of Sharia law, by its established normative provisions, to first arrive at the correct concepts of phenomena and their precise definition, and second, to prevent any collision between the rational judgments arrived at through economic analysis with the legal judgments that are characterized by totality and absoluteness.

Based on this methodological framework, we will present an analytical exposition of fundamental contemporary phenomena from an Islamic perspective as we have defined it. The goal is to arrive at contemporary rulings that interpret the methodology of dealing with these phenomena, whether in interpretation or practical approach to them.

3.1 Ownership and natural resources

Ownership is the central pillar of economic activity, whether in satisfying human consumption or in the pursuit of owning means and factors of production to ensure productive operations. Therefore, the determining factor lies in the perspective based on economic doctrine within its overall theoretical context. In practical terms, the determinants of its factors are products of social, political, economic, and cultural data existing within the society at a given time.

In liberal thought, as we outlined in the second part of this work, ownership is defined according to natural law embraced by liberal thinking. It revolves around private property that aligns with individualism and utility, which are the central tenets of this ideology. This thought emphasizes the supremacy of private property and minimizes the role of the state in the economy, or at least restricts it to a narrower scope, based on the prevailing political and social conditions in society.

In the overall, collective context, we also presented to Islamic thought in the second part of this work the issue of ownership and its legitimacy in its private and general forms as a scope that falls within theoretical wisdom while acknowledging that the practical formula takes varying partial and relative forms according to the data of the social, political, and economic reality and within the historical stages that govern the process of events. For theoretical wisdom to take on its practical dimensions according to the historical stages of formation, it must, and even obligatory, be subject to economic analysis so that its concepts and methods are consistent between the requirements of Sharia and the rulings of reason. Since our work deals with contemporary Islamic economic thought, we must analyze the issue of ownership with its doctrinal reference and contemporary forms by contemporary formative data. Thus, analysis becomes necessary to reach fair and correct interpretive rulings according to the principles of Islamic thought and in harmony with rational rulings.

In the doctrinal foundations of Islamic thought, the ownership of God Almighty over the universe emerges prominently. "For what is in the name and the earth"[217] is not a contractual issue aimed at the freedom of disposal of the owned property as it is in the practical case with humans. Rather, it is a doctrinal perspective of the divine essence that never stops at the limits of theoretical wisdom, considering it merely a theoretical matter with no practical implications, as interpreted by many thinkers, including some Islamic ones. They interpreted God's ownership as a theoretical consideration, suggesting that mankind's succession over it entails no practical consequences.[218]

We disagree with the limitations of this perspective, explaining this as follows: The wisdom of the Creator, the Almighty, lies in the goals that are sought to be achieved, and since the data of Islamic thought, based on widespread deduction and inference, the goals within this topic may be indicated as justice and rebuilding the earth.

Therefore, in the context of justice, it is not permissible for humans to monopolize, through private ownership, the acquisition of land and natural resources and exploit them at the expense of others or prevent them from benefiting from them. Land and natural resources belong to all humans currently existing and those who will be born, and they have the right to the gifts of the universe entrusted to them. Thus, ownership of land and natural resources in their general context is the common property of humanity.

In the context of "reconstruction of the earth," the conclusion we can make is the Islamic emphasis on action and making it the source of special status while defining it with boundaries that prevent exploitation of others.

---

[217] Surah Al-Baquara, verse 116.

[218] Muhammad Hussain Beheshti, *Islamic Economics* (Al-Taarof Publications, 1988), 17–18.
Ghassan Mahmoud Ibrahim and Monzer al-Qahf, *Islamic Economics: Science or Illusion* (The Contemporary Thought for Publishing, 2000), 26.

Through this, we arrive at the abstract ruling in line with the Islamic perspective and consistent with Islamic economic doctrine regarding the issue of private ownership through the source of labor, negating exploitation, and public ownership of natural resources according to formulations and methodologies that align with the historical context of each stage. Thus, within our analysis and according to the standard principles of Islamic thought and within the contexts of rational judgments, we confine our discussion on the topic of ownership to the scope of land and natural resources only in our contemporary setting.

3.1.1 Land ownership

With the beginnings of the Islamic state and during the phase of conquests, specific formulations of land ownership were implemented according to distinctive characteristics:

A. Inhabited land by humans at the time of conquest, and once conquered, becomes public property of the nation. As for uninhabited land at the time of conquest, state ownership applies.[219]

   The difference between these two forms of ownership lies in that public ownership of the entire nation should be utilized by the ruler to contribute to satisfying the needs of the nation. As for state ownership, it can be invested for the benefit of the nation through state projects for the welfare of society.

   On the other hand, the revitalization of land by individuals grants them ownership within state lands, if they pay their dues and the individual does not have the right to dispose of it, but rather the right to benefit from its resources if they continue to develop it. If they abandon their development, the land is taken away from them.

[219] Muhammad Baqir al-Sadr, *Our Economy*, 441–443.

B. Muslim land acquired through invitation without engaging in any battle includes inhabited land revived by its inhabitants, naturally fertile land, and barren land. The principle of state ownership applies to barren land, while naturally fertile land is also owned by the state. As for the land cultivated by its inhabitants who voluntarily embraced Islam, it belongs to them, and they are not obligated to pay any taxes as they were before embracing Islam.[220]

C. Lands of reconciliation refer to lands whose inhabitants did not resist Islam and did not embrace Islam but rather made a peace with Islam while maintaining their religion. In such cases, the terms of the reconciliation must be applied.[221]

In general, it is possible to return in detail to this topic through the author we referred to—namely, Sayyid Sadr. Through his work, we can infer that the overarching religious formulation of Islamic thought has delineated the paths of public ownership in its formulations as well as defined conditional private ownership. This ensures that both public and private ownership, in achieving their objectives in essence, align with the divine enlightenment sought through Sharia. This means that human stewardship is coupled with human rights that prevent any exploitation or deprivation of humans, in the sense of justice requirements, and is also linked to the cultivation of the earth as well as exerting effort through work.

Here, there is a methodological issue that must be addressed, which requires presenting the issue of natural resources before deriving contemporary rulings on land ownership. We need to discuss the religious perspective within its reference context regarding the ownership of natural resources and then proceed to the contemporary situation.

---

[220] Ibid., 468.

[221] Ibid., 473.

2.1.2 Natural resources

In the same context that we followed in presenting the rulings regarding land, we now apply it to primary materials and natural resources within the frameworks defined by Islam in absolute abstract terms. This means that succession is a right for every human being, both existing and yet to be born, over resources and primary materials, and it is not permissible to prevent or monopolize this right. The principle of justice must be applied within this context. The issue of land development is achieved through labor, which establishes legitimate private ownership, meaning the right to ownership derived from work as the price for the effort expended in developing the universe. Based on this, Islam defined—according to the prevailing social, economic, and political circumstances at that time—the ways to deal with natural resources and primary materials as follows:

- Surface minerals, which require effort to reveal their properties, are considered public property. Individuals who discover them are allowed to benefit from them according to their needs without the right to monopolize them.
- Subsurface minerals that require effort to reveal their properties and are close to the surface of the earth are also considered public property. Individuals who discover them are allowed to benefit from them according to their needs.
- Subsurface hidden minerals have two opinions: one is that they belong to the state, and the other is that they are public property.
- Natural exposed water is considered public property. There is a common saying attributed to the Prophet Muhammad (PBUH): "People are partners in water, fire, and pastures." However, water that is discovered and accessed through work and digging grants the discoverer the right to satisfy their needs without interference from others. Any surplus beyond that is for others without demanding compensation.
- As for other permissible resources or wealth, their ownership is private and acquired through labor.

In general, this presentation was presented by Sayyed al-Sadr in his book *Our Economy*, and one can return to it to view the detailed formula in a specific manner and accordance with the Sharia rulings.[222]

3.1.3 A contemporary perspective on the issue of land and natural resources by deduced Islamic standards and rulings of reason

In our contemporary reality and considering the social, economic, political, and technological developments and their data, it necessarily generates an approach, methods, and judgments that impose an economic analysis capable of reaching conclusions that align with the objectives of Sharia law and the dictates of reason. Based on that, the objectives of Sharia law, as presented above, have produced the following principles and standards:

A. The concept of succession, which is at the core of Sharia law, does not imply merely arbitrary boundaries. Rather, the successor is a trustee for humanity, both existing and future generations. This means that it is a collective ownership belonging to everyone and cannot be monopolized by specific individuals or groups. The principle of justice must be applied to benefiting from its resources.

B. The contextual presentation of Islamic Sharia law strongly emphasizes the imperative of cultivating the land. Consequently, labor occupies a prominent position, elevated to the level of worship. This necessitates rewarding such effort, thus making labor the primary source of private ownership.

C. Islamic economic doctrine, as discussed in the second part of this work, has instituted both public and private ownership. These are considered absolute and comprehensive rulings, from which derive various practical and relative

[222] Muhammad Baqir al-Sadr, *Our Economy*, 494–522.

measures, according to the socioeconomic and political realities of society.

D. The principles of dealing with partial or relative economic aspects, derived from the comprehensive theoretical context, are found in specific areas that guide Islamic jurisprudence under economic titles such as contracts, transactions, and so forth. However, our focus in this study is confined to reaching rulings within the overall context of our contemporary situation.

On the other hand, the data of reason guide us to principles and standards as follows:

A. The principle of justice is a fundamental pillar of existence. Economically, the worrying state of national economies points to the serious and destructive situation of developing nations through wealth distribution imbalance. This issue, highlighted by a deep flash, resonates in its dimensions through succession and justice. It should be a goal addressed by Islamic thought within the context of its rulings.
B. Economic, social, political, and technological developments in the world necessitate the search for divergent rulings that historically prevailed and have been applied to the issue of ownership and wealth. For example, to develop the universe, Islam legislated ownership of barren land for those who work on it, as we previously mentioned. However, this approach may not align with the contexts of technological advancement, where technology can rapidly develop vast areas within a limited time frame with sufficient capital ownership of production means. This is practically unreasonable as a justification for ownership. Another example is the issue of dealing with land ownership through Islamic conquests, which is a case no longer present in our current era.
C. The objectives of reason converge very well with the objectives of Sharia, that ownership itself is not a goal but

rather a way to provide its fruits to satisfy human needs. Therefore, the issue of the human standard of living is a goal pursued both religiously and rationally through justice in wealth distribution.

D. Productive work as a reward for human physical and mental effort is the primary source of ownership, and it also aligns reason with Sharia.

E. The level of economic, social, and political transformation and development varies among societies worldwide. Therefore, constructing economic indicators to reach accurate standardized rulings requires precision in assessing the level of development and societal interaction at the private, relative, and partial levels. Consequently, rulings addressing phenomena through the Islamic economic perspective must take this into account and reflect this reality within a Sharia-based rational context.

Based on the data we have provided, whether religious or rational, we present the following approach leading to contemporary standards with an Islamic perspective, within any existing political system in the world's societies as an Islamic intellectual position.

Based on paragraph E of the rational data we have provided above, we see the necessity of adopting an analytical economic approach to the data of each researched society. This approach should be based on the perspective of Islamic doctrine in its general form (i.e., through public and private ownership as outlined in the framework we have specified as a solid and abstract nucleus associated with a rational understanding of advanced economic data). This approach aims to achieve the highest level of justice and the highest level of resource development, including economic and human development. This can only be achieved through collaborative research teams comprised of Islamic thinkers in the fields of Islamic law, jurisprudence, Islamic philosophy, and economists possessing economic analysis capabilities. This institutionalized research effort does not exempt Islamic thinkers from individual contributions to delve into in-depth research within this context.

2.2 Cash and interest

2.2.1 Cash from means to ends

We are not here to present a historical overview of the evolution of cash usage. However, it is necessary to highlight important points as milestones in this field to provide insights into the significant role—indeed, the pivotal role—of cash in shaping economic activities.

Cash serves as a tool to facilitate the exchange of goods and services, replacing the barter system, which is fraught with difficulties and challenges in determining the equivalence between goods, storage, and deferred payment. Therefore, it is a tool that does not inherently possess value but has been given symbolic meaning—a characteristic it does not originally possess but has been agreed upon to serve as

1) a way of exchange;
2) a measure of the value of goods and services as a standard;
3) a store of value and deferred payment.

The functional role of cash theoretically imposes a neutral role, having no impact on economic activity but solely facilitating transactions. However, in practice, it has transcended this functional definition to become a determinant factor in the overall economic life. Signs that we mention here in this context are indicative of this development.

Initially, with certain commodities used as currency, their pages were turned due to their inability to perform their role as a store of value, being susceptible to changes due to nature's influence. Consequently, the world adopted the metal-based system, particularly gold (known as the gold standard system).

It's worth noting that this metal inherently possesses real value, not merely symbolic value attributed to it.

The gold and silver standard systems also inherently possess purchasing power, leading to the emergence of the gold exchange standard system, where the currency is covered by a certain amount of gold about the quantity of paper money in circulation.

The neutrality of money was a prominent topic discussed by classical economists from the eighteenth to the twentieth century. Notable among them were Fisher (1911), Robertson, and Keynes (1927). The quantity theory of money was derived from the relationship between changes in the price level and changes in the quantity of money. This theory was used to predict the observed price reactions to changes in the quantity of money, expressed as M.V = P.T, where

- M represents the quantity of money,
- V represents its velocity of circulation,
- P represents the price level, and
- T represents the volume of transactions.

International cooperation in the field of monetary policy led to successive conferences in the late nineteenth century, resulting in the idea of gold reserves as a cover for issuing credit notes (the gold standard).

What matters to us in our current study is the situation that monetary policy has evolved into, starting from the twentieth century, with the collapse of the gold standard monetary system and the establishment of the gold exchange system (i.e., starting from the Bretton Woods Agreement after World War II).

After World War II, the Bretton Woods Conference, considering the outcomes of the war, laid the foundations for an international monetary system:

A. The gold standard was established as the cornerstone of the new international monetary system, requiring countries to link their currencies to gold, meaning they had to specify a certain weight of gold for their monetary unit, without implying the freedom to exchange currency for gold.
B. Only the US dollar was exchanged for gold.

As for external reserves, this right was restricted to central banks of countries. Accordingly,

A. the cash reserves of countries became foreign currencies instead of gold. Of course, the US dollar was the primary currency convertible into gold through central banks. Instead of holding gold reserves, countries began to hold foreign currency convertible into gold, making the dollar the "currency of currencies."
B. gold no longer had a presence in domestic trading.
C. this system gave the United States immense power to manipulate monetary dynamics in its favor, allowing it to issue quantities of dollars to achieve external, political, or military investment goals, as occurred during the Vietnam War and its funding.
D. the injustice of this system lies in granting privileges to the United States. When it faces a deficit in its balance of payments, it suffices to increase the circulation of dollars, and the deficit continues without affecting its economy.
E. this system, in its external contexts, allowed the United States, through its expansion of monetary issuance, to exploit the world, as expressed by the French president de Gaulle.

This system enabled America's economic dominance, which persisted until the late 1960s. However, the lack of honoring the convertibility of the dollar to gold, frequent devaluations of the dollar, and massive expansions of its issuance led to crises and conflicts. This prompted US president Nixon in 1971 to issue a decision to delink the value of the dollar from gold. Consequently, gold became a commodity for free exchange, and the floating exchange rate system was imposed in 1976.[223]

[223] George Qurm, *The Governance of the New World* (Universal Publishing, 2013), 166.

The neoliberal ideology, with its monetary approach, served as a starting point and absence of the real economy's dynamics. The era of Reagan and Thatcher marked the globalization of market liberalization and financial deregulation. This led to the subjugation of international institutions to Western authority and the guidance of the Group of Seven major economies, which, in turn, operated under the hegemony of the US administration. This trajectory laid the groundwork for economic crises worldwide, including those of 1987, 1995, 1997, 2000, 2008, and 2009.

The analytical study of the performance context of this system directly indicates that the source of crises originates from the core of the Anglo-Saxon ideology, represented by neoliberalism and its critical approach, according to the quantity theory of money.[224] This approach sanctified monetary policy, independent of any political authority of the state. As a result, central banks began to operate without any oversight from public authorities. The consequences of this approach were evident in the economic crisis of 2008 to 2009, following the collapse of the American mortgage lender Lehman Brothers. Subsequent collapses reverberated throughout the world's economies. In contrast to the liberal ideology advocating for the end of the state's economic role, the state became the sole refuge for alleviating the effects of this crisis and navigating through it.

The performance context of monetary policy according to neoliberal thought prevailing globally, in response to American dominance, necessarily imposes at least a practical intellectual analysis based on the reference of Islamic thought as an obligation to fulfill the mission that prioritizes justice. Before addressing that, it is essential to provide a detailed exposition related to monetary policy, specifically interest, and the Islamic perspective on it.

---

[224] For a detailed understanding of the foundations of neoliberal thought and its quantitative perspective on monetary policy, you can refer to Wissam Malak, *Development of Economic Thought*, part 2, 508–522.
Also see Jonathan Story, "The Emerging Global Financial System," in *Political Economy and the Changing Global System*, ed. Richard Stubbs and Geoffrey R. D. Underhill (National Center for Translation, 2018), 345–378.

2.3 Interest and usury

The evolution of the use of money from a mere medium of exchange to an end (as we indicated above) made interest a factor for the reason of possessing money. However, initially, it is necessary to define the concept of usury and the concept of interest. Are they synonymous, or is there a complete or partial distinction between them?

Usury has been historically associated exclusively with cash since ancient Greek times. It was linked to obtaining money for consumption purposes, making it ethically unacceptable, condemned, and reprehensible, as Aristotle's famous saying states, "Money does not generate money." This rejection of usury, driven by ethical considerations, continued in the subsequent ages in Europe, across all economic doctrines. It was defined by the term "usury." The term "interest" only emerged after the advent of the capitalist mode of production in the seventeenth and eighteenth centuries. Interest was then established as a tool for obtaining capitalist loans and using them in investment operations. Legislation followed, according to the arguments outlined previously in section 11.1.1 of the third part of this work.

This indicates the distinction made between usury and interest, as well as the justifications for legitimizing interest.[225]

In Islamic jurisprudence, there is clarity about the concept of usury (riba) and its prohibition. The word "interest" never appears either in the Quran or in the hadith. Usury denotes increase and addition, and it is affirmed in two sources.

The first is in lending without any condition other than that of increase and benefit derived from it. The second is in transactions. The eminent Allama Muhammad Jawad Mughniyah compiled

[225] During my period of study at a university in Germany, and in economic curricula, the concept of usury came under the term *Wucher* and differed from the term *interest*, which came under the term *Zins*.

the opinions of the leading jurists on the subject in his book *Imam Sadiq's Jurisprudence*, and he mentioned them as follows:

- *Usury in lending.* Lending involves imposing something on someone, and the borrower is required to derive benefit from the loan. It is based on the saying of the Prophet Muhammad: "Every loan that draws benefit is usurious." Therefore, jurists unanimously agreed on the phrase "usury in lending, conditionally on increase and benefit without exception."[226]
- *Usury in transactions.* Usury is affirmed in sales with the following two conditions. The two conditions for the prohibition are that the exchanges must be of the same kind and that they must be weighed or measured.[227]

The prohibition of usury is explicitly mentioned in the Quran and is a matter of consensus among all Muslims, and it does not require further evidence: "And Allah has permitted trade and has forbidden usury."[228]

Most Islamic writings, to the extent of my knowledge, equate the concept of usury with interest. Here, I refer to an in-depth and serious study by Dr. Khalid bin Abdul Rahman Al-Mashael titled "Interest and Usury: Suspicions and Contemporary Justifications," published online, which attempts to prove the equivalence between usury and interest.

Additionally, Allama Sayyid Mohammad Baqir Al-Sadr made serious attempts to justify interest in certain specific and relative contexts.[229]

A deeper examination of the use of money within the framework of capitalist production patterns and the transformations witnessed in production processes and structural institutions, whether

---

[226] Muhammad Jawad Mughniyah, *Imam Sadiq's Jurisprudence.*

[227] Ibid.

[228] Surah Al-Baquara, verse 275.

[229] Muhammad Baqir al-Sadr, *Interest-Free Banking in Islam* (Dar al-Taarof Publications, 2011).

as companies or cartels and their financing methods through financial institutions, reveals that interest plays a fundamental role in economic events, whether developmental or crisis-generating. We observe the growing significance of money to the extent that it has become the determinant factor in the trajectory of economic development. The analytical perspective that paved the way for this role in our contemporary history is evident among the new liberals, especially the Washington and Chicago schools, where the fundamental role of a real productive economy fades away, highlighting the role of money as a determinant factor in national economies. Therefore, the liberal economic perspective of the new monetarists outlines a global capitalist economic trajectory that generates crises, with a monetary economy serving as the core of national economies where interest plays a driving role. In light of these considerations, we needed to articulate the affirmative view held by the Islamic intellectual perspective regarding money, interest, and usury.

It is impermissible, within the specific framework of this book, to engage in individual economic activities by endorsing rulings related to money, interest, and usury. Despite its specific understanding of Islamic thought and jurisprudence regarding the centrality, breadth, and depth of the subject in economic life, Islamic thought imposes the necessity of forming scientific formations that bring together economists and jurists to study the evolution of money usage comprehensively, considering all its contemporary aspects and impacts on economic reality and, consequently, its causal effect on interest.

We believe that there are partial distinctions between usury and interest, as evidenced by our assertion that financial capital is not a way of production but rather a tool, and therefore, it does not merit interest but rather compensation for its performance. (See section 11.1 of the third chapter of this work.) Thus, we conclude that there are aspects of interest applications that meet the criteria of usury and are therefore subject to prohibition, while other aspects may deviate from this criterion and thus be legitimate. This is a simple example, but the derived vision of the Islamic perspective necessarily requires striving, as we have argued, to at least conduct research or provide analytical guidance to determine how to deal with this subject, which constitutes a daily interaction in people's lives. This has been a significant factor for me to engage in this subject individually.

Conclusion

A liberal ideology that dominates most countries worldwide, driven by globalization for several decades, has led to almost absolute hegemony. It claims superiority and writes its end in history as the noblest and sole contributor to human development and progress. It has produced, for humanity, a "new man" resembling that dictated by economic theory, characterized by illusory maturity and keenness on personal interest. He is cautious, selfish, and incapable of grasping the essence of truth, nobility, or human transcendence. Western thinkers who are fair-minded acknowledge this. Is this the dream of humanity that the Anglo-Saxon thought, in its neoliberal form, has elevated, sidelining global thought and dealing with it in terms of superiority, interest, and domination?

In our contemporary reality, where seismic shifts are sweeping the world toward changing the hegemony's unipolarity and international influence, it is imperative for us, facing historical responsibilities, to present a thought that does not stop at the limits of the dangerous trajectory of neoliberal illusionary discourse. Instead, there is a necessity to propose humanistic thought from an economic perspective that is more relevant to the concerns of the people neglected by neoliberal thought and its institutional behaviors, a thought that is more rational and more connected to the economic ethics and collective morals of humanity, elevating human dignity and engaging civilly with the world's peoples. It is a thought that illuminates the path to be followed with convictions that build genuine civilizations for the world's nations.

Faced with this legitimate duty of Muslim intellectuals toward humanity and toward the Creator in their call for rebuilding existence, I call for shouldering the responsibility in fulfilling this religious obligation, represented by institutional workgroups comprising prominent Muslim economic intellectuals alongside Islamic jurisprudential thinkers. Reason is the primary source alongside divine enlightenment represented by the Sharia to comprehend the developments of human life and uphold justice in a new world where the elements of human civilization interact.

Bibliography

Amara, Muhammad. *The Islamic State between Secularism and Religious Authority*. Al-Shorouk Publishing House, 1988.

Arwi, Abdullah al-. *The Concept of Freedom*. Arab Cultural Center, 2012.

Arwi, Abdullah al-. *The Concept of the State*. Arab Cultural Center, 1993.

Baggini, Julian. *Philosophy: Key Themes*. Al Takwin Publishing House, 2010.

Beheshti, Muhammad Hussain. *Islamic Economics*. Al-Taarof Publications, 1988.

Carneiro, R. L. *A Theory on the Emergence of the State*. Akademie-Verlag, 1973.

Collins, James. *God in Modern Philosophy*. Cultural Diversity House, 2019.

Crespin, Anthony de, and Kenneth Minogue. *Figures of Contemporary Political Philosophy*. Egyptian Book Authority, 1996.

Din, Muhammad Mahdi Shams al-. *The System of Governance and Administration in Islam*. University Institution for Studies, Publishing and Distribution, 1991.

Din, Nasir al- (Muhammad ibn Hasan al-Tusi). *The Disclosure of the Intended in Abstracting Belief*. Al-Alami Publishing House, 2005.

Durant, Will. *The Story of Philosophy*. Al-Maaref Library, 1985.

Fadlallah, Hadi. *Introduction to Philosophy*. Al-Mawasem Publishing House, 2004.

Galbraith, John Kenneth. *History of Economic Thought*. National Council for Culture, Arts, and Literature, 2000.

Garaudy, Roger. *Contemporary Fundamentalisms: Their Causes and Manifestations*. Year 2000 Publishing House, 2000.

Ghazali, Abu Hamid al-. *Revival of the Religious Sciences*. Al-Halabi Library and Printing Press, 1939.

Habermas, Jurgen, and Joseph Ratzinger (Pope Benedict XVI). *The Dialectics of Secularization: On Reason and Religion*. Jadawel Publishing and Distribution, 2013.

Halatbari, P. K. *On Deportation in Development Slums*. Akademie-Verlag, 1968.

Hale, William, and Kenneth B. Taylor. *The Economy of the Twenty-First Century*. Distributed by the Center for Arab Unity Studies, 2007.

Hanafi, Hassan. *Concepts of Science: Work and Social Solidarity in Arab Islamic Thought*. United Nations, 1988.

Hani, Idris. *Our Ethics in Need of an Alternative Moral Philosophy*. Civilization Center for the Development of Islamic Thought, 2009.

Hellman, Hal. *The Problem of Population Inflation*. Al-Maaref Publishing House, 1974.

Hilmi, Mustafa. *Ethics* (www.kotobarabia). Beirut (no date).

Holy Quran.

Ibn Sina. *The Metaphysics of the Healing*. 2 vols. Arab History Institute, 2007.

Ibrahim, Ghassan Mahmoud, and Monzer al-Qahf. *Islamic Economics: Science or Illusion*. The Contemporary Thought for Publishing, 2000.

Ibrahim, Zakaria. *Human Problem*. Library of Egypt.

Ibrahim, Zakaria. *Philosophical Problems / Problem of Freedom*. Library of Egypt, 1963.

Ibrahim, Zakaria. *The Moral Problem*. Library of Egypt (no date).

Journal of Arts and Literature. vol. 3. 1951.

Kant, Immanuel. *Critique of Pure Reason*. Arab Translation Organization, 2013.

Kant, Immanuel. *Foundations of Metaphysics of Morals*. National Printing and Publishing House, 1965.

Kissinger, Henry. *World Order*. Arab Book House, 2016.

Kossmann, Peter, et al. *Atlas of Philosophy*. Oriental Library, 2011.

Kulayni, Muhammad ibn Yaaqub al-. *Principles of Al-Kafi*. 7 vols. Al-Adwa Publishing House, 1992.

Lips, Julius. *The Origin of Things*. Al-Madinah for Culture and Publishing, 2006.

Malak, Wisam al-. *Evolution of Economic Thought*. 3 vols. Al-Minhal Al-Lubnani Publishing House.

Marshall, Alfred. *Principles of Economics*. 8th ed. Vol. 1. London, 1920.

Masiri, Abdul-Wahab al-. *Partial and Comprehensive Secularism*. 2 vols. Al-Shorouq Publishing House, 2002.

Mason, Paul. *The Coming Global Crisis*. Printing Company for Publishing and Distribution, 2012.

Mill, John Stuart. *Utilitarianism*. Center for Arab Unity Studies, 2012.

Modarresi, Mohammad Taqi al-. *Islamic Mysticism*. Balagh Foundation, 1988.

Mouhajir, Mohamed Kazem al-. *Summaries of Lectures on Population Theories*. Arab Institute for Training and Statistical Research.

Mouhajir, Mohamed Kazem al-. *Theses in Comparative Economic Thought between the West and Islam*. Dar al-Balaghah, 2015.

Mughniyah, Muhammad Jawad. *Imam Sadiq's Jurisprudence*. 2 vols. Ansarian for Printing and Publishing, 2000.

Nazari, Hassan Agha. *Theorizing in Islamic Economics*. Civilization Center for the Development of Islamic Thought, 2012.

Piketty, Thomas. *Capital in the Twenty-First Century*. Economic Research Forum, 2016.

Qurm, George. *The Governance of the New World*. Universal Publishing, 2013.

Rawls, John. *Justice as Fairness*. Center for Arab Unity Studies, 2009.

Rousseau, Jean-Jacques. *The Social Contract*. Oriental Library, 2016.

Russell, Bertrand. *Authority and the Individual*. Al-Taliah Publishing House, 1961.

Sabhani, Jaafar al-. *Concepts of the Quran*. Al Bayt Foundation for the Revival of Heritage.

Sadr, Muhammad Baqir al-. *Interest-Free Banking in Islam*. Dar al-Ta-arof Publications, 2011.

Sadr, Muhammad Baqir al-. *Our Economy.* Al-Taarof Publications, 1980.

Sadr, Muhammad Baqir al-. *Our Philosophy.* Al Taarof Publishing House, 1982.

Sandel, Michael J. *Liberalism and the Limits of Justice.* Center for Arab Unity Studies, 2009.

Schumpeter, Joseph A. *History of Economic Analysis.* 3 vols. Supreme Council for Culture, 2005.

Sheha, Mustafa. *Economics.* University Publishing House, 1986.

Shirazi, Sadr al-Din al-. *Supreme Wisdom in the Four Journeys.* 2 vols. Al-Mahajjah al-Bayda Publishing House, 2011.

Stubbs, Richard, and Geoffrey R. D. Underhill. *Political Economy and the Changing Global Order.* Al-Qudsi Translation Center, 2018.

Tabatabaei, Muhammad Hussein al-. *Explanation of the End of Wisdom.* Arab History Institute, 2015.

Walid ibn Rushd, Abu al-. *The Distinction between Wisdom and Shariah from Communication.* Al-Maarif Publishing House, 1983.

Zaher, Ahmad. *Studies in Political Philosophy.*

www.ingramcontent.com/pod-product-compliance
Lightning Source LLC
LaVergne TN
LVHW090357210926
848480LV00002B/368